34

Coping With
Cross-Examination

Coping With Cross-Examination

and Other Pathways to Effective Testimony

Stanley L. Brodsky

American Psychological Association

Washington, DC

Published by
American Psychological Association
750 First Street, NE
Washington, DC 20002
www.apa.org

To order
APA Order Department
P.O. Box 92984
Washington, DC 20090-2984
Tel: (800) 374-2721; Direct: (202) 336-5510
Fax: (202) 336-5502; TDD/TTY: (202) 336-6123
On-line: www.apa.org/books/
E-mail: order@apa.org

In the U.K., Europe, Africa, and the Middle East, copies may be ordered from
American Psychological Association
3 Henrietta Street
Covent Garden, London
WC2E 8LU England

Typeset in ITC Garamond and Adobe Birch by
World Composition Services, Inc., Sterling, VA

Printer: Victor Graphics, Baltimore, MD
Cover Designer: Minker Design, Bethesda, MD
Illustrator: Margaret Scott
Technical/Production Editor: Casey Ann Reever

The opinions and statements published are the responsibility of the author, and such opinions and statements do not necessarily represent the policies of the American Psychological Association.

Library of Congress Cataloging-in-Publication Data

Brodsky, Stanley L., 1939–
Coping with cross-examination and other pathways to effective
    testimony / American Psychological Association.—1st ed.
        p. cm.
    Includes bibliographical references.
    ISBN 1-59147-094-3 (pbk. : alk. paper)
    1. Evidence, Expert —United States. 2. Cross-examination—United
States. I. American Psychological Association. II. Title.
KF8961.B758 2004
347.73′067′019—dc22   2003022109

British Library Cataloguing-in-Publication Data
A CIP record is available from the British Library.

Printed in the United States of America
First Edition

Contents

CONTENTS

CONTENTS

Acknowledgments

MANY PEOPLE HAVE CONTRIBUTED THEIR experiences, ideas, and feedback to the writing of this book. I am indebted to the following people for their assistance: Veronica Arnold-Tetterton, Michelle Barnett, Marc Boccaccini, Louis Burgio, Faulder Colby, Michael Lamport Commons, Thomas Conboy, Joel Dvoskin, Peter Ellis, William Foote, Bruce Frumkin, Karen Gold, Stuart Greenberg, Edie Greene, Michael Griffin, Patricia Griffin, Craig Haney, Karen Hubbard, Jessica Lacher-Feldman, Bronwen Lichtenstein, Robert Lyman, Linda McCarter, Jeffrey Popkin, Randall Price, Casey Reever, Susan Reynolds, Kathleen Ronan, Frank Rosekrans, Randall Salekin, Joanne Terrell, Mark Weisburg, Wendy Weiss, Alfred Whitehead, and Martin Williams.

I

INTRODUCTION

❧ 1 ❧

What This Book Is About

T HE CROSS-EXAMINATION IS WHERE our deeply felt and vulnerable aspects are located. The cross comes out of the history of jousting and battles, and out of contemporary sports activities in which one person wins and another loses—except it's more serious. For most witnesses, the cross is the time in a trial that symbolizes whether they are powerful, competent, and masterful—or whether they are weak, incompetent, and ineffectual.

When I ask participants in my testifying workshops to write down what they most fear about being on the stand, it is typically about some aspect of the cross. They are fearful of coming across as stupid. They worry about whether the attorney is going to make fools of them. They are concerned that a question will leave them stumped or that they will go blank when trying to speak of something they know. The words that they use to describe their fears reveal the emotional intensity of the situation; they speak of anticipated slowness of intellect, of embarrassment, and of humiliation. It makes no difference how much I lecture about preparation, context, situation, thoroughness, rules of procedure, or anything else. It is the fear of the devastating cross-examination that chills their hearts.

Destructive cross-examinations attempt to reveal problems with perception or memory, or sincerity or objectivity, which would justify giving less credence to the witness. In the case of experts who are permitted to offer opinions beyond their firsthand perception of relevant events, believability of their testimony is key to their expertise, which consists of their qualifications plus the reliability of their methods and procedures, and the factual and methodological bases for their opinions. Destructive cross-examination of experts seeks to reveal problems with expertise and bases of knowledge, in addition to the factors that are relevant to all witnesses. Confidence, likeability, and trustworthiness are common and essential foundations of all credible testimony.

Beyond these foundations of testimony are the subjective experiences of testimony: how witnesses think and feel about it. After all, if one uses the conclusions of judges and juries as the gauge of good testimony, one will often be discouraged. The evidence and issues in the law on which cases are decided usually draw on content much broader than the testimony of any one witness.

This book is about the psychology of the cross-examination, considered within the totality of testifying in court; how to think on the stand, which patterns of words to use and not use, what behaviors work, and how to understand interchanges between attorney and witness. This book is equally about fearfulness on the stand and mastering that fear.

Not all witnesses are fearful about testifying in court. Indeed, some experienced individuals approach court testimony with aplomb and ease. But they are not typical. Victims of crimes, eyewitnesses, and novice expert witnesses, in particular, are sometimes nearly paralyzed with fear. For all of the advantages that experts have over other witnesses, they too may be anxious in anticipation of testimony. Increasing numbers of experts are testifying, not just doctors and nurses, but professors, dentists, physical therapists, substance abuse counselors, handwriting analysts, and experts on physical evidence.

Some experts are willing to be on the stand. These scientists and professionals have work that routinely leads them into court. It is not that they are enchanted with court testimony but that they accept the witness role. Testifying is more traumatic for witnesses dragged involuntarily onto the stand. Some are defendants themselves in civil suits. Others are professionals who have been treating somebody who is a participant in a court action. The therapist is assumed to have something to say about quality of parenting, emotional damage in civil suits, possible future violence, or the nature of addictions in criminal actions, and is called to court. A subpoena was not part of the deal for counselors and therapists. Many professionals fuss, protest, hire their own attorneys, and sometimes do testify in court. Some of these treating experts simply hate testifying. Others detest it.

Why this book at this time? This book focuses on approaches to cross-examination testimony in the light of new conceptual and empirical understandings.[1] By drawing on my experiences and those of many other witnesses in court, it addresses how to broaden your repertoire of cross-examination testimony as well as how to approach and master testifying in depositions and trials. What this book does, in particular, is look at what attorneys seek to do in cross-

---

[1] My two earlier books about related aspects of testimony were titled *Testifying in Court* and *The Expert Expert Witness*.

examinations in depth and in breadth, so that both novice and advanced expert witnesses have an appreciation for what is unfolding and for specific replies. Empirical literature on assessment of expert testimony has begun to emerge. This book includes advice and applications from these research foundations.

This book is divided into three sections. The first section is the introduction to testimony and cross-examination issues, consisting of this chapter and the following chapter titled "Ten Things You May Not Know About Testifying." The second section is titled "Testimony: Narrative and Style" and discusses testimony and responding to the cross. It has three subsections: *Telling a Clear and Compelling Story, Obstacles and Pitfalls,* and *Cross-Examination Attacks and Bullying.* The narrative describes the forms and patterns in which testimony and replying to cross unfold not only to tell a story but also how to think, talk, and present the story or response in a way that promotes constructive processing of the content by the listening audience. The third section is titled "Expertise and Bases for Testimony," and it too has three subsections. The first subsection is *Professional Dilemmas and Boundaries* and describes the common quandaries of experts and their resolutions. The second subsection is *Attorney Extrapolations and Demands,* a particular genre of cross-examinations. The final subsection is *Clarity and Focus,* which addresses particular applications.

Some of the chapters are based on experiences that have been shared with me by individuals I know or with whom I have been in touch. The testimony episodes, the problems, and the resolutions of these people make up a good portion of the book. These exchanges have become good teaching lessons for me and for other witnesses, and I am indebted to the contributors for their generosity and openness. I welcome with enthusiasm your comments about your own courtroom experiences; it is a source of pleasure for me to engage in dialogues about testimony. Who knows? There may be another book on testifying coming down the road; if so, I would hope to include more contributions from readers. Please feel free to contact me about any aspect of the book or about your own experiences at the following address: Stanley L. Brodsky, Department of Psychology, University of Alabama, Tuscaloosa, AL 35487-0348 (sbrodsky@bama.ua. edu; 205-348-1920). Thanks to my readers for being such an integral part of this series of books.

A Beginning Point: Ten Things You May Not Know About Testifying

WITNESSES DREAM OF THE PERFECT RESPONSE. They want to execute what Pérez-Reverte (1998) described in his book *The Fencing Master* as his main character planned a book on the art of fencing: "[I]t was essential that it deliver a masterstroke, the perfect, unstoppable thrust, the purest creation of human talent, a model of inspiration and efficiency" (pp. 12–13). Yet, there is no unstoppable thrust, and, more relevant to court testimony, no perfect parry. Instead, testifying and fencing depend on discipline, practice, preparation, and poise.

These "ten things you may not know about testifying" were part of a presentation titled "Coping With Cross-Examination," as the Schnader, Harrison, Segal, and Lewis Invited Lecture in Law and Psychology, Villanova University School of Law, Philadelphia, February 14, 2002.

This book is written for both experienced witnesses and for witnesses who testify rarely or not at all. The content of the book ranges from modestly challenging and common courtroom situations to dilemmas that challenge the advanced and expert witness. However, this beginning chapter is oriented to the new expert witness. Ten pointers are offered as an introduction to procedures and events of court testimony.

Most Times You Do Not Testify. Many experts are filled with anticipatory anxiety, as they get progressively involved in cases. They are concerned that the trial will proceed at the scheduled date at which time there will be fierce grilling and cutting-edge challenges. Quite to the contrary, most cases for which the typical expert is retained never get to the trial stage. Many civil cases do proceed through discovery where experts do testify and are cross-examined in depositions (which may be used at trial in lieu of live trial testimony). Still, most civil cases settle. Criminal cases plea bargain. Most cases get deferred and then deferred again. Put that anxiety on hold; the case will likely be on hold, too.

Most Testimony Is Routine. Once experts finally do get to testify in the small number of cases that sift through the legal and procedural net, their experience is often a combination of relief and letdown. "No big deal" is the refrain that typical experts sing out after most of their testimony. The questioning is mundane, the scope is modest, and the give-and-take is unremarkable. Experts should strive to retain the sense of ordinariness from being on the stand rather than retain their feelings of anticipatory panic.

You Know More Than They Do. One expert who sometimes checks with me before testifying always consults her test manuals to refresh her memory about reliability and validity studies and standardization norms. Such information is generally important, but few experts are ever asked much about these topics. A few attorneys, often specializing in personal injury, family law, or capital cases, have substantial knowledge of mental health issues. Except for those relatively few, many attorneys have only superficial knowledge of the experts' fields. They probe, they may prepare a few good questions, but that is all. For a long time on National Public Radio, a fictional expert named Dr. Science[2] has proclaimed "I know more than you; I have a master's degree in science." Remember, you usually know more than they do. A lot more.

Nobody Looks at Your Shoes. Yes, experts think about their shoes and much more about their appearance. Hannibal Lector notwithstanding, few people look at your shoes with anything more than passing interest, unless you are wearing Birkenstocks without socks, your toes are pierced, and your toenails are painted with Day-Glo designs. Experts can slip into feeling such public self-consciousness about appearance that it can interfere with their effectiveness on the stand. Even rumpled clothing, eccentrically styled hair, and unusual color choices fade into the background in lucid presentations by persuasive experts.

It Really Is the Probative Stuff. Probative testimony deals with the essential issues to be decided. Experts can be supersensitive to other events that go on, from posturing by the attorneys to interruptions in the flow of testimony. A stimulus overload can take place that promotes losing track of the core of one's findings and opinions. Good witnesses see past the courtroom equivalent of jugglers, jesters, and jousters to their observations and information. Stay focused on what you know, what you have found, and what you have to say.

The Best Preparation Does Not Take Place Immediately Before the Trial. It is ongoing study and learning that makes a difference in court testimony. The witnesses who rush to prepare just before the trial are like students cramming for an

---

[2] See http://www.ducksbreath.com/index.htm.

examination—pressured by the process as well as the event and rarely well prepared. Massed learning does not work as well as spaced learning; furthermore, experts who wait until the last minute to cram have to start all over again when the next trial rolls around. It is like eating well regularly versus dieting just before you see a doctor or go to an important social event. The rush job is less effective.

You Do Not Have to Have an Answer for Every Question. A delusional way of thinking emerges in which experts—perhaps because they have been accepted as experts in court—feel they are obligated to give an answer to every question posed to them in court. Many times the attorneys are fishing and have no idea what you will say. Some attorneys are better at asking questions than thinking through the whole process. Release yourself from the internal drive to answer each and every question knowledgeably and perfectly. Nobody can do that.

You Do Not Have To Be Friendly. Mental health professionals in particular want to be liked. In professional work with clients and colleagues, and selectively with evaluees, some professionals charm, please, and form transient mini friendships. Indeed, on the stand, there is reason to believe that likeability and credibility are related. But not only is the concerted effort to be liked not necessary on the stand, it is often counterproductive. Too much smiling and too much of an effort to please compromises the expert's aura of believability. Being standoffish is not the goal, but seek some in-between point in which you are seen as human but not needy, objective but not cold.

It Is Not About Winning. Because the adversarial atmosphere is so powerful and the attorneys are so caught up in winning, experts can get overly caught up in thinking that their testimony is about winning. Make your case for the nature and specifics of your observations, which is about speaking and thinking well, rather than about winning. "Winning" has a causal link to the side that called you. Your testimony should be exactly the same as if the court retained you.

Make the Mistake That Can Be Corrected.[3] Some mistakes in testimony cannot be corrected. See, for example, the discussion of lying on the stand in chapter 22. Some permanent mistakes are making up references, guessing, and denying authentic problems in the field or in one's own work. The mistakes that can be corrected come from caution and deliberation. Reservations and qualifications about findings can be corrected through clarification; overstatements cannot.

THE MAXIM: *Fear and excessive self-conscientiousness are the natural enemies of good testimony. Preparation and realistic knowledge are the natural allies.*

---

[3] I am indebted to Stuart Greenberg for this suggestion.

II

TESTIMONY:
NARRATIVE AND STYLE

TELLING A CLEAR AND COMPELLING STORY

❧ 3 ❧

Bridges 1: Telling a Story on the Stand

WHEN CRAIG HANEY TALKS ABOUT HIS WORK and his court testimony, I am always transfixed. His talk in March 2002 to the American Psychology-Law Society biennial meeting in Austin was no exception. Haney (2002) was on a panel about death penalty cases. Following up on his Santa Clara Law Review article (Haney, 1995), he was arguing for the importance of spoken bridges between what the psychological results were for defendants and what actually happened. Be certain to tell a story that illuminates, Haney urged. Let the audience understand how the findings relate to what went on in the offense, and describe it in a way that makes sense. Tell it as a story that starts at the beginning of the person's life and let the story unfold. Present the persistent life issues and the ways the person acts within a meaningful description of factors and influences, attitudes and experiences, traumas and problems related to why the person committed the offense that is the subject of the trial. Address why this abused (or some

16

other key variable) person killed when some other abused person did not kill.

Fast forward now two weeks. With the Haney urgings clearly in mind, I had prepared a story to tell on the stand. The facts of the case were mostly uncontested. As a teenager a man had engaged in a series of thefts that led to his imprisonment for 15 years. At the age of 31, he was present with four other people when they robbed and killed an acquaintance for the large work bonus he had received. When I was called to testify, this man had been convicted of capital murder, and I was offering information that his attorneys were presenting as mitigating factors.

The defendant had taken three intelligence tests including mine at different times, and he had IQ scores ranging from 57 to the low 60s. He could not read or write. Because of his long imprisonment and time in jail just before the offense, measures of adaptive functioning were limited. My task, as I saw it, was to make clear to the jury the meaning of being mildly retarded in terms of what he thought was happening at (and around) the time of the offense and what he understood generally in his everyday life.

With the goal of being "Haney-esque," I wanted to make his experience come alive. I know a little about retardation, and I spent a day searching the databases and library for information on the subjective, emotional experience of being retarded. The databases were unproductive. The library yielded about 15 books, and I borrowed a few more. I read. I took notes. I thought about the issues. I was often frustrated at the rote repetition of the same content and how few good ideas and constructs were new to me. I put effort into being prepared.

The trial rolled around, the usual introductory aspects were accomplished of who I am, in what ways I am qualified, what I did, and what I found. Then the attorney who retained me remembered the one question I requested that he ask.

17

"Doctor," he began, "would you please tell the jury what it means to be retarded in terms of understanding what is going on around you?"

He got the question just right. I was pleased and ready. The most important parts of my testimony drew on two metaphors. I began, "You can view what being retarded means for people by thinking about partially deaf persons. They often miss much of what is going on around them. Assume they are not competent lip-readers. They will be aware that much is said around them that they do not follow. People are agreeing or suggesting or laughing at something, and some important components of it are not accessible to them."

From the emphatic head nodding from three members of the jury, I assumed some of them were hard of hearing. "What partially deaf people do is go along as best they can. They try to pass. They do not wish to state repeatedly that they cannot hear. Instead, they smile, nod, join in, and conceal their lack of knowledge about what has happened. That is just the way it goes with mildly retarded persons. Much of what is said around them is not comprehended. Words and ideas are used that they do not understand. They do their best to conceal their lack of intelligent understanding and seek to be accepted, to be part of whatever is happening, even though they follow only part of it." The examining attorney then opined that he was deaf in one ear and that was just what happened with him. There was no objection. But he asked me to explain more. I went on.

"Think of the times you have been in a room with physicians, or PhDs, or scientists when they are discussing something in their fields. They may be talking about T cells, or pathognomonic signs, or X-ray spectrography. What most people do is act as best they can to indicate they are following the conversation. In fact, when my son talks to me about his DNA mutation research with Drosophila, I follow it for a little while, and then become mostly lost, and try never to let on

18

that I am lost. That is the way it works with most people. And that is the way it works when a retarded person is surrounded by people talking about things he cannot quite follow."

From there I spoke about how one cannot tell if a person is retarded by looking at him or her. This assertion was pertinent because the disoriented, ill-kempt man who had sores on his face and torn clothing when I had interviewed him at the jail looked terrific in the courtroom. His hair had been cut, the sores had healed, and he was dressed in a new, nicely fitting suit his attorneys had just purchased for him. He was dressed better than I was, no great achievement to be sure, but other attorneys might have bought an ill-fitting, too large suit from Goodwill or from Goody's discount clothing store to make the defendant look smaller and less stylish. Then I discussed the people who could be recognized by facial or skull features—Down's syndrome and hydrocephalics—and about others who could not be seen to be retarded; the latter people were described in terms of how they sometimes could pass until they speak. Again the purpose was to provide a narrative bridge between the ways the defendant now looked—rather like an executive from the neck down—and how he was in everyday interactions.

Still one more bridge seemed to be in order. Kirk Heilbrun (2002) has described the differences in the ways risk assessments are received according to how vivid or pallid are the descriptions. Vivid descriptions enhance feelings; pallid descriptions minimize feelings. When the reports are presented in a narrative form that promotes fear or anxiety, such as stating that of 100 people, 20 will be likely to be at risk of violence, the ratings of danger are almost twice that as when reported in percentages, such as a 20% risk of violence. There seemed to be a direct connection to testifying about retardation.

The norms on the test that I used indicated that this man fell at the 0.2 percentile. It would have been possible to

19

describe the defendant as scoring at the lowest two-tenths of one percent of the general population, an altogether accurate report. Toward the aim of bridging the space between the actuarial data and the meaning for this person, I spoke of people, not percentages, in this manner. Consider 500 adults chosen at random but including the defendant. Imagine these 500 people brought together into a large room. The defendant would be at a lower level of intellectual functioning than every single one of the other 499 people.

Haney (1995, 2002) spoke of the bridges between the results and the testimony as serving to put the defendant's actions into context. In his discussion of capital murder testimony, he addressed social histories as context, beginning with the observation that it is never his role to diminish the significance of the offenses the defendants have committed. It is not excuses but explanations he seeks to share, and those explanations must include a social as well as psychological framework. Thus, the effects are interwoven of poverty, abandonment, abuse, maltreatment, institutional failure, and drug and alcohol abuse. Haney presented what he called the myth of equally autonomous "free choice." He wrote:

> Apparent choices, praiseworthy or otherwise, are not made unencumbered by past history and present circumstances . . . Particularly in the case of powerful risk factors and traumatic life experiences like chronic poverty and childhood maltreatment, different kinds of behavior—behavior that must be understood [that] as variation in adapting, coping and struggling to survive a set of circumstances that few if any have "chosen" to endure. (Haney, 1995, p. 592)

Capital trial testimony is a small part of court testimony, but these principles of telling a story that bridges the individuals with their history serve well across much mental health and other testimony. Some elements of the stories of defendants have to be shaped by history and life of the individual involved. Even persons with similar backgrounds, behaviors, and offenses have major points of divergence. Still, it is not necessary for every expert to start from point zero in creating stories. No professions are close to having a warehouse of story lines. For now, we may need to look toward what Craig Haney has given us, to create our professional banks of stories for the kinds of people we see and about whom we testify.

THE MAXIM: *Tell the story of what you have found and believe in a way that makes the technical material accessible and that enhances the jury's understanding of your opinion. Build a narrative bridge between your findings and the actual experience of the defendant or litigant so that the testimony comes alive to create a meaningful story.*

Bridges 2: Narrative Techniques for Courtroom Testimony

S OME PEOPLE SEEM TO BE NATURAL STORYTELLERS. In company, they spin out a story that grips the listeners and commands attention. Other speakers quickly lose their audiences to impatience or apathy. So it goes with testifying on the stand. On the surface, some people seem to be naturals, testifying as if they are born to it.

Yet, these seemingly natural skills can be learned, studied, and mastered, even by those who might not be good storytellers in other settings. To do so calls for patience and concentration. Think of the techniques involved in telling a professional or personal story on the stand as being directly related to traditional storytellers, authors, and singers.

To introduce narrative methods in telling a story as an expert witness, I will describe my own ways of having found a voice with the hope that it may assist other experts in thinking about how to find their own voices as storytellers on the stand. I proceed with the risk of self-indulgence. Readers with a low tolerance for self-indulgence by others should skip ahead to the next chapter.

My own odyssey as a storyteller in psychology began without much fanfare or success. My first article, written about four decades ago, was titled "Self-Disclosure in Dormitory Residents Who Did and Did Not Seek Counseling." It was a report of a little study I did at the University of Florida with residents of South Hall where I was Head Counselor. In retrospect it was a simple-minded, narrow piece that did not unfold a story in any real depth about why these residents actually sought me or somebody else for counseling. Editors of two journals had the good judgment to reject it before it finally was published (Brodsky, 1964).

Other experiences and pointed feedback eventually accumulated to help me with the narrative techniques of telling a professional and scholarly story. For example, the chair of my thesis and dissertation committee, James Dixon, returned my thesis drafts nine times before he was satisfied that it was an adequate piece of writing. He returned my dissertation drafts to me only twice, a sign to me at the time of a giant leap forward.

In the 1960s and 1970s James McConnell was editing a journal called the *Worm Runners Digest*. To be fully accurate, it was half a journal. On one side was the *Journal of Biological Psychology* about research in learning, especially with flatworms, printed to mid-issue. Then the reader would run into the last upside down page of the end of the *Worm Runners Digest*, a journal of humor and satire.

I wrote two small articles for the *Worm Runners Digest*, one called "A Touch of Sanity" (Brodsky, 1971) and the next titled "The Quiet Passing of Nough Pennix" (Brodsky, 1972).

The content is not important now (it was no more important at the time) other than the fact it got me rolling in thinking about how stories unfold.

At different times I took short courses on writing and storytelling. While serving as a visiting professor at one university, I found myself with time on my hands because the university administration accidentally closed registration for my assigned courses, except for the last five minutes, at a time when course registration was done in person in a large coliseum in which students waited in line for permission slips to get into courses. With this freed time previously allocated for teaching now available I took a course in mime, and in white makeup and tights I went out with my fellow mimes to shopping centers and malls. I was the worst mime in the troupe, but it was a lesson on how technique was central in communication. When you do not have words available, getting right to the core of the message comes pretty fast.

At another university at another time, I fell in with an aspiring writer, who reminded me "in medias res." That literally means in the middle of the thing. Start in the middle of the story, the lesson was, so that you get people caring about what happens right away, and then tell what you wish. Along with Jodi Wright, who had written a short story with the attention-grabbing title "Ted Bundy Was My Newsboy," we enrolled in a fiction writing class, and I started on a novel titled *Whistling Dixie*. The lesson that has stayed with me from these attempts at fiction writing is perseverance. Even during times when there is no inspiration to develop a narrative or to tell an interesting story, seek to do it anyway. There is nothing like forcing oneself to tell or write a story for storytelling to begin. To put it in psychological terms, the cognitions follow the behaviors. Start writing, coerce yourself to get going, and the thoughts about it develop.

Isaac Asimov had always been one of my favorite novelists, but his irreverent little books titled *Isaac Asimov's Lecher-*

ous Limericks (Asimov, 1975) were part of my schooling in
how to write and think. His lecherous limericks (the idea of
any limerick truly being lecherous is interesting—they are
mostly racy) were presented in a format of one limerick on
every other page. On the facing page he presented a narrative
of where he was and how he came up with the idea for the
limerick, which oftentimes occurred at professional meetings
or dinners with his psychiatrist wife, and just how he actually
generated the words, rhymes, and ideas. He took ordinary
experiences, events, and thoughts and wrote about them in
such a way that a clever twist appeared.

Neil Gaiman's (1999) book *Stardust* served a different
purpose. After I read this novel, I was taken with how Gaiman
put so much information of such interest in so few words. At
least, I knew it could be done, and took it as a goal in my
own reports. Some of my colleagues write reports for the courts
that range between 20 and 50 pages. Mine range between 4
and 6 pages, with the notable exception of reports of assessments of multiple plaintiffs in civil suits. The shorter the reports, the more clearly you can discard the content unrelated
to the issues of the case.

Then, when going away for a holiday, I bought the
collection *Science Fiction 101* by Robert Silverberg (2001). It
was to be pleasure reading. In addition to his 17 science fiction
stories in this book, Silverberg put together a series of essays
on how to write. As I read the essays, I found myself thrilled
at his ideas. I talked about them relentlessly and found myself
wide awake at night thinking about them. What Silverberg
did in describing his becoming a science fiction writer was to
combine suggestions about narrative that synthesized many
fragments that echoed my own efforts, and he put them clearly
onto paper.

I was going to write at this point that these observations
that follow are not mine, but rather my paraphrasing of the
principles that Silverberg developed about science fiction

writing. But they are indeed mostly my observations too. I knew that they were mine when I read them and again when I wrote them here. I have not tried to do justice to Silverberg; instead, I have recast his perspectives of narrative into what it means to be telling a story on the stand.

1. If God were an expert witness and testified enough in court, he (she) would get devastated now and then during cross-examination.

2. A good narrative has the total package: essential information, how it made a difference, the interrelated nature of the character of the defendant or plaintiff with respect to the key events, and a lucid style of presenting.

3. Tell how the defendants or plaintiffs have resolved their own conflicts and issues in their own unique ways.

4. Do not expect that you will be the Shaquille O'Neal or Margaret Atwood of testimony. It does take innate skills, but many great athletes, writers, actors, and singers have reached high levels of performance through committed effort. If you do not have what it takes now, devote yourself to getting it.

5. As you describe the nature of the person you have evaluated, explain in a way that helps along the understanding of what happened at the central event, how the person reacted, and why.

6. A lot of what you do when you tell a story on the stand will be outside the range of your awareness. Nevertheless, make rules about what you plan to do in the course of your testimony. Test them out. Revise them. Test them out again, and so on.

7. Seek out writings and knowledge on technique of testifying. Effectiveness in witnesses reflects how much they use information about narrative technique.

8. An evaluation can be perfectly, superbly conducted in the spirit of the best science and practice and still come across as bad testimony.

9. Make sense to the listener. It is not necessary for psychologists, for example, to present the details of standardizations of the tests they used. The listeners will be glassy eyed and daydreaming. Present whatever you say in a way that is approachable and sensible. Do not treat the jurors as colleagues; instead, treat them as interested lay acquaintances.

10. Find a fierce critic who will listen to your work, your preparation, and your testimony and give it to you with both barrels. Choose a critic you will listen to.

11. No matter how negative you feel personally toward other experts or parties involved in the litigation, maintain an attitude of respect and appreciation. It will allow you to enter and to leave this work with peace of mind.

12. The best testifying techniques are submerged within the content. If your techniques are visible, they are seen as just that—techniques, gimmicks, and devices. Good technique is invisible.

13. The best testimony sends the audience home informed and cleansed from resolving the conflict that has led to the trial.

14. The essential center of what you have to say may be located elsewhere than where you have looked. Do not get bound by your expectations and background.

15. Selling your services (through salary or fees) only means that you know how to sell your services. It does not mean that you are a successful witness.

16. It is a career-long process to get better rather than it occurring in a single moment of insightful attainment.

Consider that you never really get good enough, just better, and that occurs only if you put what you have learned to the best possible use.

17. "Technique is merely a means to an end, and in this case the end is to convey understanding" (Silverberg, 2001, p. 50).

18. There is no single secret to testifying. Rather, "you just go on, doing your best, living and reading and thinking and studying for answers, using everything you've learned along the way and hoping that each new story is deeper and richer than the one before" (Silverberg, 2001, p. 50).

There may be no other area in the health professions about which practitioners worry more and do less than court testimony. Anxiety can get in the way of doing anything. What I suggest here is serious effort, that is, intentionally devoting a piece of your personal and professional life to improving how you think and speak about what you do. It may spill over into other aspects of your work. Let us hope so. But at least you can learn to tell a jury a compelling story about what you know.

◻

THE MAXIM: *Treat the understanding of narrative technique in testimony as a serious and substantial undertaking with personal discipline, increased awareness, and systematic practice. Then tell your story.*

◻

❧ 5 ❧

More Yin, Less Yang

IT IS NOT UNUSUAL FOR WITNESSES to say too much while on the stand. Anticipating where a line of questioning will lead, they seek to cut off the varmints at the pass, or some other similar prevention–intervention metaphor. It works this way: The witnesses are fiercely eager to prevent cross-examining attorneys from trapping them. As a result, the witnesses overdo it. They are asked a question which may be answered simply. Instead, the witnesses bound forth with fierce and overblown verbiage. An anticipatory defensiveness is mobilized.

The alternative is to assume a presence of calm receptiveness and controlled answers. The calmness is communicated by the totality of the personal manner and behaviors. Think of the most peaceful and serene person you know. Recall how that peaceful person is able to allow anything or any statement to come her or his way. Capture for yourself what it would be like to be that perfectly calm and comfortable no matter what questions are asked on the stand. Be ready

29

to answer just as much as you choose: not too much, not too little. When the moment feels right for expounding and explaining, then you expound and explain. In the meantime, listen well, receive readily, and do not rush to fill all possible space in the attorney–witness dialogue.

After hearing me speak about these approaches and seeing me demonstrate them in the safe sanctuary of the workshop, Randall Price tried it in court. This is what he wrote about his experience:

> The case I recently testified in involved a clear traumatic brain injury. I was retained by the defense and did a neuropsychological evaluation that evidenced dysfunction. The key difference between my judgment and that of the plaintiff's expert (who wanted to treat the plaintiff for the rest of his life) was that I thought the plaintiff could engage in some kind of gainful employment and that it would be good for him if he did. By the way, the plaintiff himself agreed with me. A vocational expert who was also retained by the defense followed with testimony detailing what kind of work the plaintiff could do.
>
> The Zen experience (which I attribute to your Austin workshop) was that I testified with more yin than yang. I said less than usual. The plaintiff's attorney subsequently followed my brief answers with more open-ended, softball, "why" questions that let me give a narrative to the jury. The jury liked it. I felt more in control than ever. I had been a little worried about my testimony because the plaintiff's attorney was not very experienced or adept, and I feared the experience of playing racquetball with someone who just started playing. My deposition had gone that way, but the trial was great.[4]

---

[4] Randall Price, personal communication, May 4, 2002.

One can understand yang testimony as being like the tennis games of Serena Williams or Leyton Hewitt: aggressive, attacking, starting off with fierce first serves and continuing with hard ground strokes scattered around the court (Wimbledon was on at the time of this writing). In tennis, the technique works well. In court testimony, however, the cross-examining attorney always serves, in the sense of asking the questions. The witness is much more in the role of waiting, preparing a good return of service. Years ago, Harold Solomon was known on the professional tennis circuit for his relentless defensive game, always chasing a ball down. A good witness is ready to spot the ball as it approaches, to keep a sharp eye on the ball, and to move in position to return.

The yin equivalent is waiting with care for the question and giving a controlled, modest reply.

Consider this: "Isn't it true that the sources of information you have drawn on are necessarily limited and flawed?" A yang reply, a Serena Williams answer, would be to pounce on it, and assert that information is neither necessarily limited nor necessarily flawed, but is "a representation of multiple sources of converging data that serve to identify, confirm, and reconfirm working hypotheses before they are accepted as conclusions." It would be an aggressive, attacking response. A yin reply would be "No." Then the attorney is faced with the dilemma of following up with an open-ended question such as, "What do you mean, no?" That allows the witnesses to run with the answer as much as they choose.

As much as there are both attacking and defensive tennis players, there are witnesses whose nature leads them to be attacking or defensive. Consider the possibility of adding a yin posture to your repertoire. Unlike so many other patterns of responding, it never comes across as a gimmick or ploy. Try having this calm receptiveness as an available option. Do not say everything you might say when the moment arises.

31

From a position of emotional calmness, give a clear, solid, simple answer. Save yang for when you need it.

THE MAXIM: *Do not make automatic, aggressive, controlling yang replies to all aggressive questioning. Use some calmer, simpler, receptive yin responses.*

❧ 6 ❧

Imagery to Reduce Anxiety

EXPERIENCED WITNESSES KNOW WHAT TO EXPECT in their physical environments. The waiting areas for witnesses are familiar to them, as are the locations of quiet areas, restrooms, and coffee availability. In one courthouse I frequent, the clerks to the judges always have a full and fresh pot of coffee available for expert witnesses and attorneys. Waiting for morning appearances in court is made easier by the coffee and the warm interpersonal reception in the judges' outer offices.

In the same manner, experienced witnesses know where to look when they enter the courtroom. Instead of the wide-eyed, frightened deer presentation of nervous witnesses, experience teaches them to scan the courtroom easily, and then look immediately ahead along the way to being sworn in and then to the stand. Not only does the trip to the witness stand repeat a recognizable experience both physically and mentally, so does being seated in the witness chair become a known experience.

Courtrooms have particular identifiable markers and many basic similarities. Much like surgical staff in operating rooms and psychotherapists in therapy offices, experienced witnesses find that they quickly settle into the physical environment of the courtroom, ready to address the overall task at hand and the anticipated questions.

With first-time and inexperienced witnesses, it is quite another story. Little about the setting is familiar. Some of them have never been in a courtroom before for any reason. Still other novices have been in courthouses only for personal reasons in roles unrelated to their work. They worry about their first appearance on the stand. Several coping possibilities are present, one of which is the use of imagery for managing oneself in this unfamiliar setting. First-time expert witness Mark Weisberg wrote to me of his experience.

> As I stood waiting outside the courtroom I felt what I would assume was normal anticipatory anxiety. After all, this was my first forensic case and my first expert testimony in court. I noticed that the room was somewhat dark, with dim florescent overhead lighting. The walls were paneled in dark wood. The whole scene reminded me of Manny's Steak House here in Minneapolis, an old institution where old guys would cozy up with a 32-oz. Porterhouse and a cigar. This spontaneous association made me chuckle a little.
>
> After entering the courtroom, I took a seat and waited for the attorney to call me. I looked at the scene: judge seated up high on the bench to my right, plaintiff and defense attorneys on either side, and the court reporter situated directly in front of the judge, at my level. As I looked a second time at the court reporter, I realized that he looked exactly like Burt Bacharach, the 1970s composer of such hits as "Raindrops Keep Falling on My Head," "I'll Never Fall in Love Again," and "Do You Know the Way to San Jose?" As a part-time jazz musician, the sometimes touching,

sometimes quirky Bacharach songs have always had a special appeal to me, and I have played them often. The notion of this famous composer of '70s hits preparing to record my testimony was so amusing to me that it took everything I had not to burst out loud with laughter. Any remaining anxiety immediately disappeared. My testimony went well.[5]

Not all novice witnesses should expect the appearance of a vivid image or association to someone in the courtroom, or for the emotional equivalent of raindrops to start falling on their heads. Yet, such associations do occur. Sometimes a juror or attorney reminds me of a close friend, a beloved relative, or an eccentric colleague. At other times, a person in the court has eyes that sparkle with an expression of serenity and good will, and I have thought of mentors who extended themselves to me in approving and kind ways.

With equal frequency, members of the jury bring associations to my current or former students. The association that Mark Weisberg had to a familiar restaurant in his home city would be unusual for me, but I may have spent too much time in courtrooms for this image to appear. Nevertheless, the common element that appears in these situations is a sense of positive connection. This reaction makes things easier and better for the testimony and for the witness personally.

One can seek to create reassuring imagery, as well. Memory training seeks images that permit memorizing long strings of words or people's names. It takes a commitment to develop images and the mastery of this skill. Once you see Marge Simpson, Tony Soprano, Frodo, Shakira, Marilyn Manson, Spike Lee, and your Aunt Effie in the courtroom, it can

---

[5] Mark Weisberg, personal communication, November 5, 2002.

help you to feel that you are in a psychologically familiar milieu and to testify well.

THE MAXIM: *Use imagery as a tool to gain a sense of familiarity with the courtroom in order to ease anxiety and enhance your narrative style. Seek to feel positively connected to the people in the courtroom and to the physical place itself.*

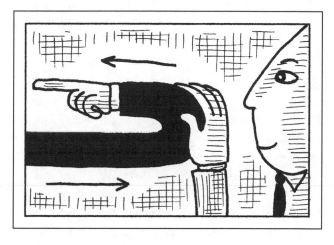

Reversals

REVERSALS IN GENERAL MAY BE UNDERSTOOD as a turnabout in beliefs, ideas, or approaches. That is, reversals flip over some common view, so that White people can appreciate what it is like to be Black, so that the powerful and privileged understand what it is like to be powerless and underprivileged and vice versa, so members of in-groups can appreciate what it is like to be members of out-groups. At their best, reversals can serve as tools to teach or enlighten.

Gloria Steinem has been a master of reversals. Her essay "If Men Could Menstruate" (Steinem, 1995) depicted with humor the ways in which menstrual periods would be reconstructed and valued if they were part of men's regular experiences. Steinem wrote:

> What would happen . . . if suddenly, magically, men could menstruate and women could not? The answer is clear—menstruation would become an enviable, boastworthy, masculine event: Men would brag about how long and how much. Boys

> would mark the onset of menses, that longed-for
> proof of manhood, with religious rituals and stag
> parties. Street guys would brag ("I'm a three-pad
> man"). (p. 367)

Steinem developed similar reversals in her "discovery" of the work of the imaginary Dr. Phyllis Freud. In the chapter "Freud as a Woman," Steinem (1994) turned on their heads the deeply seated comparative assumptions about men's and women's sexuality.

In a similar sense reversals may be understood in the courtroom (and deposition) roles of expert witnesses and attorneys. Thinking about such reversals is not easy, but for that matter, neither is it easy to consider men as menstruating. The assumption addressed here is that during cross-examination, the attorney attempts to lay traps to reduce the expert's credibility and effectiveness, while the expert, in turn, attempts to slip out of such traps. Good attorneys pursue the setting of traps by means of nonverbal communication in the form of tone and volume of voice, posture and gesture, and the phrasing of a sequence of questions. When traps work, witnesses find themselves in the position of offering inconsistent or ineffective testimony in an indecisive manner.

Most witnesses see themselves as helpless in such situations. They attribute all of the direction of the examination to the attorneys, while they, the experts, are simply responsive and, to a large degree, passive. Although often true, this situation is not universally present. Attorneys are not as clever and do not act with the cogent forethought that experts may believe. More to the point, occasionally reversals occur in cross-examination. Let us turn to one example.

In the 1990 film *My Blue Heaven*, Steve Martin plays Vinnie, a second tier mafioso testifying against a mob boss in a murder trial. The cross-examining attorney has drawn Vinnie out in court about the benefits Vinnie receives in the witness protection program. Vinnie acknowledges that he has been given a home, and a regular pay check. Then comes the reversal—the trap by the witness. Vinnie adds "that's not all." The attorney bites at the bait and triumphantly asks what else he gets. With pained tone of voice, Vinnie speaks of never seeing his mother, losing contacts with his friends, and the loss of his identity and life as he knew it. He concluded that, yes, he is testifying only because he is in the witness protection program, but it is the truth, anyway. That transformative moment moved the jurors to accepting Vinnie's testimony as untainted and truthful.

The bait is similar that expert witnesses sometimes place to entice attorneys along a particular direction of questioning. Witnesses will offer a qualified answer, saying "that's mostly so" or "the research literature appears to support this conclusion." When the attorney then asks a follow-up question about the ways in which a witness statement is only mostly so or only appears to be supported, the witness is ready with a professional, lucid, and compelling explanation of the ways in which some conclusion is mostly true, or with a substantive, scholarly analysis of the appearance and presence of a conclusion.

This reversal in which witnesses rather than attorneys set traps should be used with care. Witnesses should use it only occasionally, so they are not seen as playing games. They should use it only if they are at home in the courtroom. And they should use it only on topics which they have genuinely and fully mastered.

A final question that might be posed is whether it is proper for witnesses to use such reversal gambits. It is not for everyone. Reversals of this sort should be seated with integrity in the nature of the witnesses' knowledge and findings. Remember as well that attorneys do not have to follow up on a hint or a bait statement. They are responsible for what they ask, just as witnesses are responsible for how they answer.

THE MAXIM: *Witnesses may choose to reverse the customary process in which attorneys set conceptual or linguistic traps for them. Such reversals should be offered only in the context of thorough preparation and consistent testimony.*

❦ 8 ❦

Position and Alignment

I T WAS A BUSMAN'S HOLIDAY. With the pleasure of a block of time unexpectedly free, I spent the day in court watching three forensic experts testify about their results. They had all conducted autopsies of a 2-month-old child allegedly shaken to death by the defendant, his father. The testimony was technical and sometimes inaccessible to me (and to the jury), so I found myself watching the posture and the bodily alignments of experts on the stand.

The courtroom had a conventional setup. The witness chair was to the left of the elevated bench, and further to the left the jury chairs were arranged in two rows perpendicular to the witness box and bench.

The first expert witness sat at a 45-degree angle in the witness chair from the beginning. His body was lined up so it faced to his left, and his head and shoulders squared off directly toward the middle of the rows of jurors. He leaned forward, head and arms slightly in front of body. As the opposing attorney asked questions, this witness kept his body aligned to the jurors, but rotated his head and neck so he was looking at the attorneys as the questions were asked. Then, for all answers, both brief and extended, he swiveled his head back in line with his body and spoke to the jurors.

Without question, he engaged the jurors. However, the discrepancy between his body angle and his head and neck direction had a peculiar quality. His head rotated right and left as if he was watching a tennis match. It was distracting. My assumption is that this experienced witness had been told many times that he should look at the jurors when he spoke, and that he was carrying a good idea to an extreme.

The second witness had rarely testified. He walked to the witness chair and dropped himself gracelessly into it like a full sack of books drawn rapidly by heavy gravity. His arms hung immobile and his face was expressionless. His body faced toward the questioning attorneys, but with so little animation that I found myself thinking of an automobile crash test dummy with a weight problem. He may have been compensating for his nervousness by freezing in place. His answers were often double negatives (i.e., "that lab test elevation would not be inconsistent with severe trauma"). From beginning to end of his testimony, there was no shifting in his seat, no looking around, no movement or gestures, a blank facial expression, and little variation in tone of voice.

The third expert was more animated than either of his predecessors. He moved around a little, gestured often, and looked at the attorneys as he listened and at the attorneys and jurors as he answered. His body was mildly relaxed. His head was aligned straight on his neck and shoulders when he spoke to the attorneys. However, when he looked to his left at the jurors, he tilted his head about 30 degrees to the right and spoke very fast. His head tilt drew my attention so that it was sometimes hard to follow him.

Of these three witnesses, the first expert who was aligned directly with the jurors was the most effective. He had a sense of reaching out to the jurors; he spoke clearly at a medium pace and in understandable language. They obviously liked him.

I sat next to a physician and occasional expert witness who had also come to watch the expert testimony that day. We were certain that neither of the last two experts had a good awareness of how they sat and aligned themselves. The first expert had insight, except about the head swivel. Many witnesses do not know how they sit or what messages are communicated by their body angles and postures. Instead, they focus on the substance of what they say to the exclusion of attending to how they deliver it.

Witnesses who commit themselves to improving their performances should look for opportunities for directed feedback about what they do. The preferred vehicle for such feedback is to videotape the testimony, whether in depositions, mock trials, or the occasional live trial in which videotaping is allowed. These videotapes should be reviewed in the company of a knowledgeable observer of the behaviors that persuade or distract—someone who can discuss how the witnesses have presented themselves. Watching alone is not advised; even persons used to viewing video and audiotapes of themselves tend to cringe.

Once the problems are identified, experts should practice alternative presentations, again followed by directed feedback. At its best, this process allows witnesses to put the manner of presentation on a desirable autopilot, so that the heading and attitude are noted, corrected when necessary, but not foreground enough to be preoccupying.

THE MAXIM: *How you position and align yourself on the witness stand influences how your testimony will be received. Seek directed feedback on the direction of your body and positioning of your head while listening and while speaking in the courtroom.*

❧ 9 ❧

Witness Preparation and Videotape Feedback

For HOURS WE HAD BEEN WORKING to prepare this defendant to testify in her forthcoming capital murder trial. We were isolated in a barren meeting room in the county jail of a small rural county. Her attorneys had taken turns playing defense and then prosecution examiners as the defendant went through a practice run of being on the witness stand. The trial was coming up in a few weeks, and after three years of health problems and depression while in jail awaiting trial, she was now having her first real taste of what might happen.

As part of assisting her in communicating her story, I periodically stopped the run-through to give her feedback. I told her:

> You are at your best when you tell your story directly. Try not to drift off so much onto unrelated topics when you are answering specific

questions. Pay attention to your shoulders. Your shoulders are level when you carry on a normal conversation, but when you testify, your left shoulder drops low, and your right shoulder rises toward your right ear. That distracts the listener. See if you can stay more level. As you speak, the bottom of your lower back slips forward in the seat, and you begin to slouch. It makes you look personally reluctant and emotionally distant. When the slouch begins to happen, keep your bottom scooted back in the seat and your lower back pressed against the back of the chair. Slouching gives an appearance of sloth. Sitting more upright helps in every way. Don't emotionally disengage as you speak. Keep in good contact with the questioner and the people on the jury and in the courtroom.

The defendant was able to incorporate each of these steps for a brief time. Then, her responses would again drift, her shoulders would slant, her back would slouch, and her manner would become preoccupied. I would remind her as gently and encouragingly as I could, and she would hold the new behaviors for a few minutes. Finally, with fascination, she watched on the camcorder screen the video playback of herself in this mock examination. We went over what she did well and what she did not do well. She murmured affirmatively and nodded. We resumed.

Now, she was good. She was very good. Her posture stayed excellent, so that she looked slimmer and more involved. She stayed on subject. She showed an emotional contact that I did not know she had. We scheduled a refresher meeting the evening before her anticipated testimony, but the foundation for credible testimony was established. She was much better: believable, personable, and focused.

Many attorneys routinely seek to prepare their clients for testifying. Marcus Boccaccini (2002) has published a comprehensive review of witness preparation techniques, goals, and knowledge, in his article titled, "What Do We Really Know About Witness Preparation?" A number of trial consultants conduct just this preparatory work. Dr. Phil (McGraw) made his entrée to the Oprah Show and then to his own television program through preparing Oprah Winfrey to testify in a civil trial alleging that she had defamed the beef industry. Yet much of this work is seat-of-the-pants, shoot-from-the-hip training based on intuition and personal judgment. As part of his doctoral dissertation and other writings, Boccaccini (2002, 2003) found little solid scientific foundation for witness preparation. As a result, he developed and studied a model he called Persuasion Through Witness Preparation (PTWP).[6] Let us look at what he did.

First, working with a Public Defenders Office, he videotaped a practice run of actual felony defendants answering direct and cross-examination questions asked by their lawyers. I joined him in evaluating the strengths and weaknesses of these defendants' testimony. Next, he used the tapes to show the defendants and discuss with them the problems in their testimony and ways to address them. Finally, they did another practice run with similar questioning.

In the second part of his research, Boccaccini asked undergraduate students to describe instances in which they had been unjustly accused of some act. All were videotaped during an initial mock direct and cross-examination about their accused behaviors. Half received witness preparation training before a second examination, and the other half just showed up for a second videotaped examination.

---

[6] Marc Boccaccini completed this work under my supervision as chair of his dissertation committee. However, the term supervision hardly applies because this project represented his vision, his original thinking, and his efforts.

The control group showed no improvement. Except on one measure of self-rating their own nervousness as less, they showed no changes in testimony delivery skills, credibility, or guilt likelihood. However, there were significant positive improvements in the prepared defendants group in the forms of improved posture, gaze, quality of responses, politeness, and appropriateness of legs apart or together. Furthermore, there were significant patterns of less fidgeting, less uncertainty in answering questions, and fewer vocal pauses. The data offered compelling evidence that the training made a difference.

But all was not rosy. On two measures the prepared "defendants" were worse. They became stiffer in their posture and less animated physically, apparently as a consequence of being more self-conscious. The overall effectiveness of the preparation was evaluated using expert raters blind to whether the "defendants" were in the control or preparation groups, and whether the taped sessions were first or second (pre- or postpreparation) sessions. Preparation and videotaped feedback did indeed make a significant difference. Although more postural stiffness was observed, defendants were seen as being more credible and less likely to be guilty after training involving video feedback. It is worth noting that this research is in its early stages and more needs to be done. That said, what should the case study of the woman being prepared to testify and the Boccaccini research mean for you?

- Do not assume that you are insightful about how you would come across in court. Try videotaping yourself. You may be surprised.
- Seek out more than one preparation session.
- Draw on expert guidance about nonobvious aspects of your self-presentation.
- Use video feedback to help learn about and shape your testimony style.
- Be careful about getting too self-conscious in manner and appearing too unspontaneous.

There is more to witness preparation than obviously meets the eye. For first time or infrequent witnesses, do not take for granted that you know what you are doing. And for experienced witnesses as well, do not assume that experience means mastery. Doing something often is not always the same as doing it well. Everything I have learned about house painters illustrates the principle that experience is not the same as skill.

One more related issue is what jurors would think about defendants or other witnesses prepared for testimony. In a random sample telephone survey of 488 Alabama residents, only 18% reported they would have a lowered opinion of defendants whose lawyers had helped them give more understandable testimony (Boccaccini & Brodsky, 2002). Another implication came out of this survey. Citizens expected an innocent defendant to be at least somewhat nervous; thus, witness preparation should allow the existing nervousness of witnesses to be at least somewhat visible.

◙

THE MAXIM: *Unless you have had a remarkably good record of testifying in court, seek out witness preparation advice and video feedback to promote awareness, effectiveness, and credibility.*

◙

Hypercorrect and Personal Speech

O F THE FOLLOWING PAIRS OF WITNESS STATEMENTS, which seems better to you?

> A. Since I was not aware of my location, I could not tell which direction the vehicle was coming from.
> B. Since I was not cognizant of my location, I could not ascertain from which direction the vehicle was coming.

> A. I know not where the original paperwork was stored.
> B. I don't know where the original paperwork was stored.

Marc Boccaccini suggested these topics and generously summarized the relevant research studies. Veronica Arnold-Tetterton assisted in critically examining the literature.

A. This approach uses the most recent norms.
B. This approach utilizes the most recent normative data.

These examples represent use of hypercorrect testimony and a parallel use of ordinary language. Hypercorrection itself is usually defined as a misfire attempt at prestigious communication that takes the form of too much linguistic information or of status-oriented pronunciation (Giles & Williams, 1992). Hypercorrect speech bends over backward to be formal, correct, and impressive, so that the testimony comes across as stilted and unnatural. Hypercorrectness overapplies or misapplies words and rules of grammar. In the examples given here, the hypercorrect statements are B, A, and B.

The first of the examples of hypercorrect statements is drawn directly from William O'Barr's (1982, p. 152) book, *Linguistic Evidence.* O'Barr observed language use in 150 trials and then asked 42 Duke University undergraduates to rate witnesses speaking in a formal manner and a hypercorrect style. The witnesses using hypercorrect speech were judged significantly less convincing, less competent, less qualified, and less intelligent because their language seemed to stretch beyond the content of what they said.[7]

Courtroom testimony is more formal than ordinary conversation, so it is normal to speak more formally. Indeed, one hopes that witnesses will shape the words and form of their testimony to the setting. However, this setting is an instance in which something worth doing is not worth overdoing. This sense of overdoing it can be seen in the following contrasting pairs of parallel testimony prepared by O'Barr; the first

---

[7] In at least one other study, the negative effects of hypercorrect speech were not compelling. See Parkinson (1981). Little current research is ongoing on this topic.

statement is hypercorrect and the second statement is simply ordinary courtroom formal language.

> *Hypercorrect.* I can't definitely state whether the lights or the brakes came first, but I rotated my head slightly to the right, and looked directly behind Mr. Norris, and I saw reflections of lights, and uh, very very very instantaneously after that, I heard a very very loud explosion, from my standpoint of view, it would've been an implosion because everything was forced out like this, like a grenade thrown into a room. And uh, it was, it was, terrifically loud. (O'Barr, 1982, p. 152)

> *Formal.* I can't definitely state whether the lights or the brakes came first, but I turned slightly to the right, and looked directly behind Mr. Norris, and I saw some lights, and uh, immediately after that, I heard a very loud explosion, like a grenade thrown into a room. And uh, it was, it was terrifically loud. (O'Barr, 1982, p. 156)

The more unnatural the speech patterns are to the speaker, the less likely the testimony will be convincing. Thus, people who usually speak in lower-class language patterns will have more disastrous efforts to be overly formal. This principle was illustrated by the characters in the Damon Runyon short story, *The Idyll of Miss Sylvie Brown,* as well as the subsequent film made from that story, *Guys and Dolls,* in which gambler–criminals use an exaggerated form of proper English. They underachieve their goals by overdoing their words, expressions, and language; in this localized dialect, people are always saying *do not* when the word *don't* would do. The failed upward aspiration of speech is illustrated in this excerpt from the Damon Runyon (1944) story, *The Lemon Drop Kid*:

> And of course if a guy whose business is telling the tale cannot find anybody to listen to him, he is greatly handicapped, for the tale which a guy tells is always about how he knows something is

> doing in a certain race, the idea of the tale being that it may cause the citizen who is listening to it to make a wager on this certain race, and if the race comes out the way the guy who is telling the tale says it will come out, naturally the citizen is bound to be very grateful to the guy, and maybe reward him liberally. (Runyon, 1944, p. 453)

Is it appropriate for educated, professional, and upper-class witnesses to use overly formal language, compared with the spoken language of their audience? If such formal language is what they normally speak, it may be their best choice. The rule is, do not be something you are not. But what happens with naturally occurring overly formal speech? It presents the possibility of putting off the listeners, a risk that needs to be matched against the risk of the artificial alternative of talking down in an unnatural manner. Still, academics should use their normal and routine words and language, including passive voice when it fits. It increases credibility (Hurwitz, Miron, & Johnson, 1992).

Now we move to the related topics of personal pronouns and of referring to oneself in testimony. Examine the following pairs of sentences and, once again, choose the statements that appear to be more effective.

> A. In my best judgment, I believe that the plaintiff was being careful and conscientious when he spoke to me last June.
> B. The plaintiff was being careful and conscientious when he was evaluated last June.

> A. Ms. Harbin was in considerable distress.
> B. I think Ms. Harbin was in considerable distress.

> A. The outside persons presented conflicting and confused reports.
> B. I found that the outside persons whom I interviewed presented conflicted and confused reports to me.

The better answers are the ones with fewer personal references, that is, B, A, and A, respectively. Some witnesses spend much of their time on the stand saying *me, me, me*, in a variety of ways. I did this, I think that, I observed such, and I decided something else are common prefixes in testimony and especially in expert testimony. Research data from actual transcripts of both criminal trials (Parkinson, 1981) and civil trials (Parkinson, Geisler, & Pelias, 1983) indicate that fewer self-references may be better. Parkinson (1981) concluded that "defendants who used more markers of courtesy or deference, spoke in more grammatically complete sentences, and used more polite forms were most often acquittal (sic). Unsuccessful defendants, those who were convicted, made more references to themselves in their testimony" (p. 31). In Parkinson et al.'s (1983) study of rescripted excerpts from civil trials, the defendant was asked, "When did you first realize you were going to hit David?" The unsuccessful reply was, "I saw him coming over the hill on the wrong side. I tried to swerve but we couldn't help hitting" (p. 19). The successful response was, "He was coming over the hill on the wrong side of the road" (p. 19).

The implications about self-references for expert witnesses as well as lay witnesses and defendants are similar. Ownership of one's conclusions can be helpful, but within defined limits. Do not talk too much about yourself, and do not use first-person pronouns too much. It comes across as self-preoccupied. It is common to be self-conscious and a bit self-preoccupied when testifying.[8] However, it is visibly showing the self-focus rather than staying visibly with the task at hand that is the problem.

---

[8] Think of the Ambrose Bierce definition of egotists as persons more interested in themselves than they are in me.

The Maxim: *Do not overdo it by trying very hard to speak correctly and properly on the stand, and do not overuse "I think," "I believe," and other personal references.*

❧ 11 ❧

Metaphors in Testimony

MY GRADUATE STUDENTS IN THE BACK of the courtroom giggled all at once. Straight-faced, they had observed me while I went through the three hours of a direct examination that had been organized clearly and logically by the attorney who had called me to testify. Now the cross-examination was well underway, fueled with high-octane questions prepared by the JD–PhD consultant retained by the other side.

The cross-examining attorney asked why I had not weighed heavily one piece of collateral information that had not been consistent with my conclusions. I had replied that I looked for multiple sources of confirmation for each of the hypotheses that I developed, and there had been no confirmation for this single indication. The attorney pushed again, insistently demanding that I acknowledge I had chosen intentionally not to use this information.

"That's right," I replied. "One swallow doesn't make a summer."

56

What broke up the observing students at this point was my use of the "one swallow" proverb taken from a commonly administered intelligence test. The meaning of this proverb is that seeing a single migrating swallow arrive at its summer habitat does not mean that the summer season is present. Instead, one needs to see many swallows to accept their migration as a sign of summer.

This proverb requires a high level of abstract reasoning to solve. The cross-examining attorney may have understood what it meant, but she went blank for a second. Then she dropped this line of inquiry and went to other areas of questioning.

She could have stayed with the topic and delved into the applicability of the metaphor. Suppose she had thought more quickly on her feet or was personally knowledgeable about swallows, and asked any of these questions. How would you answer them, based on your personal knowledge?

1. Challenging the metaphor: "Isn't it possible that the arrival of one swallow can be seasonally significant in its own right?"

2. Becoming concrete: "Are you talking only about Capistrano?"

3. Becoming even more concrete: "Are you referring to the song 'When the Swallows Come Back to Capistrano?' "

4. Contaminating the metaphor: "Isn't it true that, much like psychology, the prediction of the return of migratory birds is far from an exact science?"

Possible responses:

Question 1. The best way to reply is to answer from a knowledge base about swallows, including how they travel in large flocks, and that when they arrive it is clear and unequivocal. For people who do not have such a knowledge

57

base, two alternatives are present. First the admit–deny, which is:

"Although I cannot speak as an expert to the seasonal significance of one swallow, I can speak directly to how insignificant and isolated the statement was by the defendant's Uncle Jake."

The second alternative is to let go of the metaphor. One might say:

"I did not intend for a second to make a literal statement about swallows. If you had that impression, I need to correct it."

Concrete Questions 2 and 3. Similar to working with concrete clients in psychotherapy, these questions are best answered by first acknowledging them and then moving to general principles. For example:

"I am speaking neither about Capistrano nor songs, but rather about the principle that outlying bits of data should not be given much weight."

Question 4. The contaminated metaphor. Of the several options for answering questions like this, the most appealing may be the one that addresses how truly inexact are most physical as well as social sciences. I know just enough about the physical sciences to be able to answer:

"Even in fields as apparently exact as physics, there is inexactness in the methods and knowledge base. So, yes, it is true for psychology. I assume it is true for predictions of bird migrations, although that is outside my expertise."

A last comment is in order, and that is to note the reasons I chose that particular metaphor while testifying. Part of the reason for a particular metaphor in court testimony is to keep in mind the whole audience in the courtroom, not just jury and judge and attorneys. A metaphor can enable a witness to translate technical or peripheral information into language the average person can understand. That plain language rationale has the potential for allowing a witness to communicate better and more credibly and to be less vulnerable.

THE MAXIM: *Metaphors can clarify and simplify technical parts of testimony. Challenges to metaphors are best met by defining limits of the metaphor and by placing it in an illustrative context.*

OBSTACLES AND PITFALLS

Pretentiousness

WITNESSES OFTEN ASK WHAT WENT WRONG when they were on the stand. Their backgrounds were usually good. The evaluations and content were frequently first rate. The testimony seemed to go okay, but it did not sit quite right. The jury went the other way, as well. Many factors can account for the jury not agreeing with experts, including attorney skills and weight of other evidence. However, one factor in credibility of testimony worth examining is the implicit attitude of the expert, a manner of self-presentation not easily accessible to awareness. Among competent expert witnesses, specific ways of being pretentious are especially off-putting to jurors and hard to assess personally. Sometimes it is a way of talking that communicates a message of talking down to jurors. Sometimes it is vocabulary. The sense of self-inflated worth that is pretentiousness may be thought of as the totality of behaviors, language, gestures, attitudes, and self-references. A general rule is that pretentious people do not know they are that way.

They do know that in certain situations people selectively dislike them or distance themselves for no apparent reason.

How do we get perspective on the extent to which we are pretentious? I write "we" because all of us should be open to the possibility that we are one of *them*. Remember, pretentiousness is disguised to the pretentious—their own pretentiousness is hidden. Other people's pretentiousness may seem apparent. One answer to promoting awareness is that we need aid in self-discovery of pretentiousness and its mirror image, false modesty. Sometimes accurate feedback from valued and kind others helps us from keeping ourselves too grimly committed to our importance. A sense of humor about our work helps.

Pretentiousness may be gendered. My women friends remind me that it is very male to be pompous. Although men do not have a corner on the market, we do seem to be more prone to self-aggrandizement than do women. However, pretentiousness also tends to be job related. Professors and health professionals are particularly susceptible, although professional athletes can give us a run for our money.

It is a demanding and mean task to learn about one's pretentiousness and change it. The first step already noted is to draw on wise people you know. Seek out insightful colleagues and acquaintances who have themselves sought to give up self-inflated importance, because they can guide you. Ask them to listen to your public presentations, in court or otherwise. Request that they give you their observations on exactly what elements are distracting, about how less educated people might think you are talking down to them. From this feedback, prepare a list of changes to undertake.

From that point, the feedback process becomes replaced with a continuing personal assessment of pretentiousness. Listen to how you speak of your work with noncolleagues. Intentionally introduce changes in tone of voice, in sentence length, in complexity of ideas, and in vocabulary. Use less jargon and that means becoming aware of how much of your testimony is laden with jargon. For most of us, professional jargon becomes automatic and routine. Use fewer polysyllabic words (of course, the word polysyllabic is polysyllabic—never use it in court). Check once again with your valued colleague how well you are doing. Tape-record yourself before you start and again along the path, and see what differences you can observe. Do not allow yourself to become overconfident—an issue that is the topic of the next chapter.

THE MAXIM: *Pretentiousness is endemic to professional work. Check whether and how pretentiousness may impair your credibility on the stand, and enlist the aid of an insightful colleague to change it.*

❧ 13 ❧

Overconfidence

I T WAS ONE OF THOSE DEFINING MOMENTS in the trial. A student and I were taken with the expert's mastery, knowledge, and compelling testimony. As I would learn later, an experienced investigator watching in the courtroom was equally taken.

In this puzzling murder trial, much of the evidence and the bases of opposing arguments were over the interpretation of complex and unclear information from various sources. The information was sufficiently complex that a physician on the jury independently concluded that all of the experts were wrong, and tried unsuccessfully during the trial to present his own written conclusions to the judge so that no more time would be wasted.

The expert on the stand was poised, absolutely confident and certain, and with surgical precision he cut through all of the confusing issues of cause of death and sequence of psychological and physical events. What had been a muddle before became transparently clear. This courtroom-experienced and nationally known forensic expert's solution solved the problem.

When his testimony was over, the student and I burst into the corridor, unable to restrain ourselves any longer. We bounced down the corridor, outside the courthouse, and to the car, talking effusively about the way in which this witness had resolved the case. How, we bubbled, could any juror not be convinced by him? Even the sleeper, the juror who was asleep more often than not during the testimony of other witnesses, was alert and attentive. We ran into a few other people who had been following this highly publicized trial, and we told them that we thought that the outcome was now ordained and the defendant would be acquitted.

The jury deliberated for 27 hours before the judge declared a hung jury and ordered a mistrial. A few jurors held out for conviction. But the hung jury itself was not what startled me.

I interviewed three of the jurors afterward. The remaining jurors were tearful and shaken by the deliberations, and chose not to talk about what they thought. The three jurors all said that no one on the jury believed anything said by this expert who had so convinced me.

"Why didn't you believe him?" I asked.

They answered that he was too certain. His opinions were too absolute. One juror who was a nurse told me, "There are no absolutes in knowing what happened." Some jurors were skeptical of him because he was paid a great deal of money. They believed, instead, another expert also called by the defense, a person who was ordinary, and to me, not convincing.

In posttrial discussions, I came to believe that the expert who had persuaded me was too distant. As good as he was with laying out facts, he was nowhere near as good in making contact. Indeed, when I met him briefly before the trial, I found

66

it hard to make personal contact, which is not a characteristic occurrence for me.

The high fee probably should have been addressed during the beginning of the direct examination, to inoculate the jury against it as a possible taint. However, the more important conclusion is that excellent knowledge is not good enough. Excellence in delivering that knowledge in a personal way that reaches jurors is every bit as important.

THE MAXIM: *High quality in expert methodology and opinions must be accompanied by effective delivery to make a difference. Do not be seen as overconfident.*

14

Smug and They Don't Know It

IN THE RANDY NEWMAN SONG, "I'm Dead," after the singer observes that he has been performing the same songs the same way on stage for 30 years, the chorus rings out with

> Oh, he's dead, and he don't know it!
> Oh, he's dead, and he don't know it!

So too it goes with witnesses who are smug when they testify. Smugness on the stand is first cousin to overconfidence and refers to a defensive refusal to admit limitations to what they do and know; the presentation of self is as complacently satisfied. They may come across as excessively convinced of the correctness and completeness of their work. This appearance of superiority and complacency is visible to others and hidden from self. The Randy Newman lyrics may be paraphrased to read:

> Oh, they're smug and they don't know it!
> Oh, they're smug and they don't know it!

Smugness competes with witness credibility. You may recall that credibility is positively associated with confidence, likeability, and trustworthiness. The smug witness is not liked, and trustworthiness lessens.

In individuals for whom smugness is a character trait, changing this presentation of self is difficult. It calls for corrective interpersonal experiences and intensive feedback, both best offered within the framework of psychotherapy. The paradox is that smug persons, comfortable in their insulated self-satisfaction, are unlikely candidates to enter psychotherapy unless important events go wrong in their lives.

For purposes of testifying in court, let us consider smugness as primarily situational and induced by the demands of testimony and other stressors. Few people are smug as a persistent way of relating to others; it is transient smugness that is more easily malleable, and which is the present concern.

Smug answers appear in specific cross-examination or deposition contexts. Let us look at the "Wouldn't more (of something related to your work) have been better?" inquiries. That is, the line of questions that attorneys sometimes ask is about whether more might have been done by the expert in arriving at a conclusion. The "more" questions often include whether there would have been better foundations or more useful data if the expert had:

- Spent 40 hours instead of 4 hours in the evaluation.
- Given the MCMI and PAI in addition to the MMPI.[9]
- Interviewed many more persons who had long-term opportunities to observe the evaluee.
- Had access to (more) personnel, employment, school, or medical records.

---

[9] Millon Clinical Multiaxial Inventory (MCMI; Millon, Millon, & Davis, 1994), Personality Assessment Inventory (PAI; Morey, 1991), and Minnesota Multiphasic Personality Inventory (MMPI; Butcher, Dahlstrom, Graham, Tellegen, & Kaemmer, 1989).

- Watched the evaluee personally for dozens or hundreds of hours in his or her natural environment.

A predictable response appears when experts are asked these questions on the stand. No matter how reasonable the query, the experts repeatedly deny that it would have made a difference. They state that their evaluations were complete, that everything that should have been done was indeed done, and that more time, more tests, more collateral sources, more records, and more observations would have made no difference—no difference whatever. Even when the queries are posed in a gentle and matter of fact tone and style, experts deny the worth of "more" information. This denial is so widespread and so uniform that it is almost normative.

It backfires. Although experts hope to present themselves as assured, they go one step further and actually present themselves as smug and professionally dogmatic. That is a problem. What they typically say in response is:

A. It would not have made any difference if I had more time.
Q. But aren't you always faced with time constraints that limit what you ask and do?
A. I did a complete evaluation and did everything I wanted to.
Q. Could you have gathered more useful information?
A. No. None whatsoever.

What should witnesses do to avoid being smug? Some specific replies to these more-information questions could be:

"More time might have been useful."

"Even if the other tests duplicated the results I already had, giving them would have done no harm."

"Although more complete employment records would have been useful, the results based on the information I had were clear and compelling."

"Certainly having somebody observed for every moment of their waking lives gives much more information."

Q. And couldn't that have made a difference?
"Because no observation was undertaken, or could be, there is no way of knowing for certain. My conclusions were based on my evaluation."

The more-of-everything questions may probe into the education, training, experience, and skills of the expert. There will always be some training course the expert will not have had. There is always some experience one has not had, whether in personal contact with people like the defendant or plaintiff, or life exposure to particular kinds of people, crises, harm, or offenses. In all such circumstances, begin with a comfortable awareness of this pattern of questioning. Then admit readily what you have not done. Listen attentively to the question so you know just what is being asked. Affirm the worth of what you have done while accepting the reasonableness of what you may have not done.

THE MAXIM: *Avoid being a smug witness by acknowledging that you do not know everything, have not done everything, and are constructively willing to address more-of-everything questions.*

15

Suspicion-Evoking Testimony

ASSUME TWO WITNESSES HAVE GIVEN identical testimony. Through an unlikely quirk of coincidence and events, they have been the same—or at least equivalent—in appearance and clothing. The statements they have made and their responses to questions are word-for-word the same. Yet one witness has been believed and the other witness has not. What accounts for the difference?

The differences between people we believe and trust are often not obvious. Think of specific people you have met whom you immediately and fully trust (or want to trust). Such people have ways of relating and presenting themselves that touch something positive and affirming in others. Think, as well, of particular people you have met who evoke instant distrust and suspicion; these are people who put you on your guard. They do something that makes you watch carefully that you do not reveal anything overly personal, perhaps that your credit cards are not carelessly available, or certainly that you do not accept them as possible allies or friends.

For the moment forget whether the people in the trusted group are truly honest and trustworthy, or whether the latter individuals are not. It is their impression formation that is of interest. Few people want to elicit an impression of suspicion and distance. I write "few" because there are individuals who are abrasive and negative as a means of keeping others away from intimate or even casual impersonal contact (Davis & Brodsky, 1992; Willshire & Brodsky, 2001). Suspicion-evoking people evoke undesirable outcomes on the witness stand. Behaviors that witnesses are unaware of can form such distrust and suspicion. Consider this excerpt from the novel *Shadow Puppets*.

> But as Petra listened to him, she became more and more uneasy. (He) was lying about something. The change in his manner had been slight, but after spending months observing every tiny nuance in Achilles's demeanor . . . , she had turned herself into a very precise observer of other people. The signs of deception were there. Energized speech, overly rhythmic, too jovial. Eyes that kept darting away from theirs. Hands that wouldn't stop touching his coat, his pencil. (Card, 2002, p. 128)

As adept as the lead character Petra in this excerpt may have been in picking out deception, she had a head start. She knew a great deal about the man she was observing, and most of it was bad. When jurors watch a witness testify for the first time, there is no history. That is, the testimony is the first time they have seen this person, the first time they have heard this evidence, and the first time, for the most part, that they have been in this particular evaluative context.

In another sense, it is not the first time. It is common for me to be told by strangers that they know somebody who looks exactly like me who lives in Des Moines, Detroit, or Delaware (especially Delaware). As the conversation drifts to that look-alike, it becomes clear that some generalization of

73

emotion extends toward me from the feelings about the look-alike. The generalization is communicated strongly if these are positive feelings. Negative feelings are less clearly communicated, but I sense they are often there as well.

This process applies to many other people. A friend from Australia has had strangers from around the world approach her and start speaking German in the belief that she looks so German, she must be German. A man with facial deformities has described how people speak slowly and loudly when they first meet him, in an apparent and inaccurate assumption that he is intellectually dim. On occasion, people speak in an overly and unnatural academic manner after they have learned I am a professor of psychology. They assume I am going to be a critical judge of their psychological sophistication.

Few of us know the true full impact of our physical, occupational, and social selves on others. Nevertheless, you can count on people reacting to you and assessing you from preset judgments based on subtle as well as obvious elements of who you are.

Let us go back to the four components of behavior that made Petra in the excerpt feel that the speaker was being deceived:

- Energized and overly rhythmic speech.
- Too jovial.
- Eyes that kept darting away.
- Hands that wouldn't stop touching his coat, his pencil.

The first of these behaviors is not supported in the nonverbal communication literature as an indication of deception. However, the other three components are supported at least in part. If strangers are happy or jolly beyond what the situation warrants, we may question their motives. Too much or too little eye contact elicits beliefs that the person may have something to hide. Excessive touching of clothing or self, called *adapters* in the nonverbal communication literature, is interpreted as a sign of anxiety, which, in turn, is often interpreted as an indication that something is being hidden.

To this point, our concern has been the eliciting of suspicion by professionals who are trustworthy. It is instructive to look at the mirror image, that is, the eliciting of trust by individuals who are not trustworthy. Frank Abagnale (1980) described just such successful evoking of unmerited trust in his autobiography, *Catch Me If You Can*, later made into a motion picture. Abagnale successfully impersonated a college sociology professor, an airline first officer, and a physician, among other poses. He attributed his successes to the following factors he identified as common to con artists. They are: ". . . well-dressed and exude an air of confidence and authority. They are usually, too . . . charming, courteous and seemingly sincere" (p. 129). Furthermore, Abagnale stated, they carefully observe what is happening, down to fine details, and research with care what they are attempting to do.

In the same sense, it is altogether reasonable for lay and expert witnesses to seek to impersonate the knowledgeable person they hope to be on the stand. Many professionals have an imposter syndrome, anyway, in which they feel far less able than their credentials and achievements indicate. To see if it aids in effective presentation of self, witnesses should experiment with simulation of confidence, authority, and poise. It is not for everyone because it can interfere with being one's authentic self, but it is an option worth exploring as part of learning about and shaping of the presentation of self.

Most individuals avoid feedback about their stimulus value unless there is a reason. Learning to be a psychotherapist or a public figure are two such reasons. Preparing to testify in court is another. The pre-20th-century phrase for describing a person whose behaviors are unpredictable and destructive is the loose cannon rolling about on the deck of the ship. Until you get clear awareness of the impact you have on others, and particularly of possible patterns that evoke suspicion or distrust, then your own statements, appearance, and gestures may be a similar hazard. Here are three examples I have observed:

- One former athlete turned health professional displays a snarl when given a tough cross-examination.
- A former model dresses in sexualized clothing on the stand.
- An altogether giving and warm man speaks in a listless monotone when he testifies.

To find out whether you evoke suspicion or distance calls for a concerted effort. Few people have a realistic and clear understanding of their surplus value, beyond the words, of how they come across.

◾

THE MAXIM: *Check whether any aspects of your behaviors, appearance, or gestures make jurors suspicious, and if they do, seek to eliminate those aspects.*

◾

❖ 16 ❖

Visible Displays of Emotion 1

WHILE IN THEIR MOTEL ROOM, the defendant explained, he had been kissing the six-foot tall woman who had picked him up in her car. His buddy was sitting on the other bed, talking to the woman's equally tall female companion. In a flat tone of voice, with minimal description, the defendant explained that the woman—he always called her the large woman—had started playing with his penis. He put his hand under her dress, discovered a penis there, and realized the large woman was, in fact, a man.

This small young man stood 5 feet 4 inches tall and weighed 120 pounds. He mumbled as he testified, and at times, it was not possible to understand what he was saying. Still, the essence of his story was this: While walking on the street, he and his friend had been picked up by the two women, mutual flirting ensued, and then they all went to the motel. After he discovered that his female companion had male genitalia, he insisted that they all leave. Instead of dropping him off at his house as promised, the two transvestite men continued to drive. His friend escaped by leaping from the car. According to the defendant's testimony, the men referred to him as their little bitch, and drove on. He attempted to get out of the car, and got one leg outside, but one of the men still held him tightly. At that point, the defendant took out a pistol and shot several times, killing both of the abductors.

From the beginning the defense attorneys knew they needed the defendant to testify on his own behalf, and, further, they knew that they would have a problem. He not only mumbled and spoke in street language, but his emotions were invisible. A speech therapist was retained who sought to help him with his clarity of speech and language use.

For those of us watching him testify on the witness stand, it was apparent that he was doing poorly. After all, he was speaking of events that most people would find seriously distressing. He described his discovery during sexual play that his presumed female companion was a male. He then reported what happened while he was trapped in the car being driven to some unknown place as they made sexual remarks to him. These events would be disturbing at the least, and, more likely, catastrophically frightening to reasonable people.

The way he spoke of the events, however, was with minimal description and little detail. He reported what happened without any sense of just what led up to each step, and without communicating much of what transpired. The more important omission was his lack of emotion. He indicated the discovery of the male sexuality of his companion with the same emotion one might use to mention that his car needed washing. When he related the attempted kidnapping and his efforts to get away, he spoke in brief, bland statements.

What he did not do is communicate emotionally the essence of what had been pieced together by his attorneys and others; that he had been terrified. Because of his small size, because of the discovery of the companion's male genitals, because of the inability to get out of the speeding car, he feared he was going to be assaulted. For this defendant to be effective on the stand, he needed to have a visible display of emotion. Instead, he presented the nervousness of testifying but no fear, no distress, and no intensity in his narrative.

Why did he not show these emotions? Here are four hypotheses: First, by his nature he avoids emotional displays. It was a product of his personality, his upbringing, and the well-ingrained values of his peer group. Even more than most other men, he could not readily access his inner experiences. Second, for this 21-year-old man, 2 years had passed since the incident. A large part of his adult life had passed since the shooting, and the emotional memories had faded. Third, he had been in jail for 2 years, and the jail experience itself had been so full of adjustment difficulties with other inmates that he had shut down internally as a means to cope. Fourth, he had told this story so many times and to so many people that he had become habituated to it and desensitized to the emotional content.

He needed to display emotions to be effective on the stand. His inability to be emotional was especially seen when his attorney asked: "Were you terrified for your life?" The defendant replied "Yeah" without convincing this observer.

His failure to be emotional is reflective of a broader pattern that one sees with witnesses. There are times when some element of visible emotion is important to believability. Similar to Carl Rogers's theory (1942, 1951) that emotional congruence between therapist and client is responsible in part for therapeutic change, emotional congruence between content of testimony and accompanying emotion of the witness is important for influencing jurors' opinions.

For expert witnesses, the issue is somewhat different. Experts are expected to be subdued in emotional displays because their roles call for them to be objective. Objective roles call for detached emotions, up to a point. Emotional empathy and concern in small doses go a long way toward indicating that the expert witness is a real, feeling human being. Jurors are alienated by mechanistic expert witnesses who present their material in an overly intellectual manner. Yet, even good expert testimony has to be muted and context appropriate.

Two problematic extremes of displays of emotion may be identified. First are the excessive displays, in which the expert witness engages in dramatized presentations. In some cases, witnesses sprinkle their testimony with words such as *horrible, heinous, unthinkable,* and *ghastly* while their tone of voice and facial expressions indicate disgust or repulsion. Of course, witnesses may be testifying about events that are indeed harmful or distressing to the parties involved, however, expert witnesses compromise their own impartiality when they demonstrate emotionality through tone of voice or choice of words. Highly emotional displays suggest the witnesses are emotional and therefore partisan. Moderated expressions are better received.

The second problem is with witnesses who are excessively detached. Some experts are chillingly cold and unfeeling as they talk about emotion-eliciting events. Although excessive detachment is preferable to excessive emotionality, both extremes reduce credibility.

Some experts are by nature emotionally demonstrative or detached. What should these experts do on the stand? Testimony backfires if witnesses try to be something they are not. The strain of pretending to feel (or not feel) an emotion leaks through, and observers may judge them negatively. A preferable choice is to moderate the display of either extreme. Highly emotional people should dial it down a few degrees. Very cool and detached people should let existing and underlying feelings be a bit more visible. The goal is to stay true to one's characteristic style while modulating the display.

THE MAXIM: *Displays of emotions should be moderate, should be consistent with one's natural style, and should fit with the context about which one is testifying.*

❧ 17 ❧

Visible Displays of Emotion 2

IT IS NOT UNUSUAL FOR LAY AND EXPERT WITNESSES to be shown photographs of victims of violent crimes. These photographs sometimes show dead persons, gaping wounds, internal organs, entry and exit sites from knives or bullets, or other evidence of major injuries. It is a routine part of the case for the prosecution to use graphic photographs to make the reality of the violent act more vivid to jurors and sometimes to witnesses.

Attorneys defending an individual charged with violent crimes often ask how jurors would react to such photographs. Would the jurors be distressed? Would they look away? Would they become so emotional that they would be less able to process evidence in a reasonable and objective manner? Would they be pushed toward finding the defendant guilty to insure that someone is punished for this violence?

Little attention has been paid to how witnesses respond to seeing such photographs of blood and victims and to how

82

witnesses answer questions about their reactions to such photos. Attorneys who ask such questions may attempt to diminish the credibility of witnesses by portraying the witnesses as either too subjective or as too detached. It is these attempted portrayals that we address here. Consider these questions.

> Question 1: Doesn't it make you absolutely sick when you think of Ms. Jones having her throat cut this way and nearly having her head cut off?
>
> Question 2: Aren't you totally disgusted when you consider these children who have had their whole lives taken away from them?
>
> Question 3 (In civil trials): Doesn't it make you want to throw up when you hear of a large man in power assaulting and sexually pawing a vulnerable and fragile woman?

The aim of attorneys who ask such questions is to lead the witness to acquiesce to the equivalent of a tabloid headline ("Yes, it *is* horrible when farm children are probed by drooling alien kidnappers") or to get expert witnesses to come across as unfeeling. The latter goal may seem especially reachable because expert witnesses who have been exposed to many bloody photographs and scenes typically react with more distance than the average person.

When confronted with questions about such incendiary photographs or other content, listen with attentive care to the actual question asked, and then be honest in replying. Once those states of attentiveness and honesty are attained, some additional principles apply. For experts who ponder possible reactions to such questions, earnest professionalism will often serve well. Thus, two possible profession-oriented answers to the above questions are:

> Answer 1: Nothing in my work makes me disgusted or sick.
>
> Answer 2: I make a point of emotionally detaching myself when I take on my work

83

assignments. It is an essential part of being objective and scientific.

Note that both of these above examples identify the work role or responsibility of the witness. It is not about being detached as a person. Rather, it is the professional or scientific context that allows the witness to be objective. Nevertheless, such answers may not be satisfactory for all witnesses. A responsive choice for individuals who are more genuinely emotional is to speak to the broad issue and not the molecular questioning. Thus, a witness might offer a reply similar to one of the following:

> Answer 3: Whenever a person loses a life, I am saddened.
> Answer 4: It is chilling to see the harm that one person can do to another.

All four of these replies have in common that the witness is not led or provoked by the attorney. Narrative answers are given, instead of a yes or a no response. When emotions are acknowledged, they are done so in a calm and measured manner. The witness rephrases the issue in terms that make sense for his or her role and the work involved. The witness slips the trap of excessive empathy and can present emotionally neutral answers.

THE MAXIM: *Visceral images and sensationalistic questions may be met best with attentiveness and honesty, as well as professional detachment mixed with moderated empathy.*

❧ 18 ❧

Repetitions

JUST AS GREAT WITNESSES can give much power to their testimony through well-crafted words, so can poor choices of
words and phrases diminish the power and significance of
testimony. Witnesses may present problematic repetitions of
phrases that lead to louche testimony. *Louche* means being
not straightforward but rather being shifty and disreputable.
Consider this example of Aldus Huxley (1937) using *louche* in
his novel, *Crome Yellow*: "There had seemed to be something a
little louche in the way she had suddenly found herself alone
with Ivor" (p. 182). The book *Crome Yellow* itself dwells at
times on the power of words, the issue discussed here in the
context of testimony. Huxley (1937) put it this way:

> "Words," said Denis at last, "words—I wonder if
> you can realise how much I love them . . . the
> feeling of magic, the sense that words have
> power. . . . With fitted, harmonious words the
> magicians summoned rabbits out of empty hats

and spirits from the elements. Their descendants, the literary men, still go on with the process . . . trembling with delight and awe. Rabbits out of empty hats? No, their spells are more subtly powerful, for they evoke emotions out of empty minds. Formulated by their art the most insipid statements become enormously significant." (pp. 215–216)

In the following examples, look at how word usage can diminish testimony, and specifically at how repetition of phrases and words compromises credibility. Linguistic scholars have developed methods of measuring the amount or variety of word use, which is part of word repetition.

One can measure the repetition of words in any language sample through what is called the type to token ratio, or the ratio of different words (types) to total words (tokens) in any sample of language. If a person uses 70 different words in any 100-word sample, the type to token ratio (TTR) would be 0.70. There is reason to believe that lower TTRs are generally worse for witnesses because, within most contexts, purposeless repetition (lower TTRs) on the witness stand leaves a negative impression. Carpenter (1990) has found that deception and evasive manipulation make their way into language in the form of more repetition, that is, lower TTRs.

Phrase repetition, in particular, can be examined in testimony in the case the media titled "Grandmother Hires a Hitman," the Ann Trexler trial, which was held in February 2002. The defense attorney for Ms. Trexler was examining Kim Miller, a key witness for the state who had made a deal with the prosecution. That agreement was being discussed, along with the suggestion that the witness had compromised the truth of her statements to avoid imprisonment. At the excerpted point in the testimony, the deal was raised. As you read the edited transcript, note how less effective the phrase, "I don't know who wouldn't have," is when used the second time. Also, observe how excessively compliant the witness appears.

Defense: This, uh, convicted felon issue, you're now a convicted felon on a third degree felony, correct?

Kim Miller: Correct.

Defense: And that's much different than being a convicted felon on a first-degree felony punishable by 30 years in prison is it not?

Miller: I'm not really aware on how all those sentences and guidelines go, but if you say so, yes.

At this point Ms. Miller makes a serious error. Witnesses should never automatically acquiesce to a statement made by the cross-examining attorney. Miller could have said she did not know and then stopped. She could have left out the last phrase, "If you say so, yes," and allowed her otherwise adequate reply to stand. Or she could have said, "Of course."

Defense: Well, you were first facing a first-degree felony that would be punishable by thirty years in prison, correct?

Miller: I wasn't aware of the thirty-year imprisonment, but I knew it was a serious charge, yes.

Defense: Truth is, you thought it was life, didn't you?

Miller: Twenty-five to life is actually what I thought.

Defense: Yeah, and later on you thought that that charge was about to be upgraded to a first-degree murder, principal to first-degree murder, correct?

Note that from here forward the witness gives three passive agreements in response:

Miller: Correct, Uh-huh.

Defense: And you were going to be taken before the grand, or your case was going to be taken before the grand jury, correct?

87

Miller: Uh-huh.

Defense: And that you would be then facing a charge that carried execution or life in prison without parole just like Ms. Trexler is facing today?

Miller: That's correct.

Defense: And that's when you moved into gear and with your lawyer, made the deal.

Miller: I don't know who wouldn't have.

The cross-examination goes now into the plea bargain details signed by the witness, which was read aloud by her.

Defense: So you have this safety net that no matter what, in any way that you violate probation, if you do anything in violation of your agreement with the state, after you are sentenced here, you had an agreement that no other charges could be filed against you arising from this incident?

Miller: Correct.

Defense: So, you are no longer touchable for murder, the worst you can get is 5 years for violation for probation, that's the way you understand the deal, isn't it?

Miller: I guess.

The "I guess" reply falls into the category of evasive and shifty. It has a reluctant quality to it. In such a situation, she would have been better off saying, "Yes, that is exactly how the arrangement works."

Defense: That's the deal you wanted wasn't it?

Miller: I don't know who wouldn't have wanted that deal.

Here the repetition of the phrase washes away the value of her answer. Because she said almost the same thing a few minutes earlier, it sounds as if she is relying on an automatic reply. The repetition handicaps her credibility.

When a video of these exchanges was shown to a group of my graduate students who investigated effectiveness of courtroom testimony, they muttered and moaned as she testified. They found themselves aware that her recurring delivery of slippery words made them skeptical of this witness, as did her excessive agreement with the attorney. The problem of saying the same thing again in testimony can be illustrated by thinking of an expert witness making any of the following statements two or three times during testimony: I don't know anything about that. The data do not provide an answer. I am certain that is what my data conclude.

The more the witnesses change the wording of similar responses to questions, the less the witnesses appear to be empty automatons. Some questions during cross-examinations and depositions do repeat themselves. Thus, some answers will go over ground already covered. The effective witness, however, changes the emphasis or word use, or may say, "As I indicated in reply to the same question you asked me a few minutes ago, what I observed was . . . ."

THE MAXIM: *Do not repeat the same phrases and words without a clear purpose; otherwise, your testimony may appear to slide into a style that seems automatic or evasive.*

❧ 19 ❧

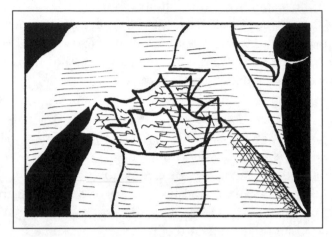

Pocket Men and Quarterbacks

AN OUTGOING AND AFFABLE PSYCHOLOGIST sought me during a break, and he explained that he would appreciate a little of my time. "I am embarrassed to talk about it," he said to me, "but I have a terrible problem testifying in court." I offered to speak to him then, but he said that would not be good. I suggested that we set aside 10 minutes during the next break, but he said he needed something more. So, the next morning we met over breakfast, with an hour set aside for this apparently urgent matter.

> "The problem," he explained, "is my memory. I just can't remember any of the things you said I should know. I can't remember studies. I can't remember numbers. I can't remember coefficient alphas. I can't remember dates. I can't remember test results or what my clients have said. Sometimes I get wiped out when I am testifying in court. I try not to testify, but my job requires that I get called."

I asked some of the obvious questions. Had he suffered any medical conditions, such as a stroke, that would have caused the problem? No. Had this been a recent problem? No. Did it interfere with his ability to function in other capacities as a psychologist? No.

His concerns had been heightened by what I had said during the workshop. He was fully in agreement that one needed good preparation, needed to know the literature, needed to research the applications and limitations of tests and interviews, and needed to master the knowledge that would make him a visibly competent assessor and witness. However, his ability to reach these goals was another matter, and he judged his ability as severely lacking.

The customary mode I advise for expert witnesses is to study and memorize the scholarly and professional foundations of their work. One may consider that these skills are related to the work of a group of 19th century entertainers called *pocket men*. The men would go about on public streets and challenge passersby to name any small object. Once the object was named, the men would instantly produce the object from somewhere in their voluminous pockets, after which they would be given a small coin in appreciation.

Part of their success was in knowing the base rates of items that would be named. The second part of the success was a concentrated attention to organization of objects within their many pockets and to memorizing what objects were where. That approach is how I see testifying. It calls for much preparation, knowing the base rates of likely questions, organizing all of the content in a careful and systematic manner, and committing as much as possible of the important research, methodology, and assessment findings to memory.

Yet, the distressed man speaking to me could not serve as the witness equivalent of a pocket man. For some reason— and I do not know why— he was not able to memorize content that most other expert witnesses can. It is not that other experts

91

have perfect recall. Indeed, under the pressure of intense scrutiny and questions, even experts with good memories may have recall problems.

The model that may be seen as an alternative to pocket men is what football coaches do to call plays to quarterbacks. The quarterbacks have the play codes written on tape wrapped on their wrists. Sometimes the plays are written there because of the complexity of the plays and signals. Sometimes they are written there because the quarterbacks have difficulty memorizing the playbook.

My suggestion to the psychologist with the poor memory was that he should prepare detailed written outlines of background issues in the literature and current issues and case findings. Then he should keep them directly available in a manner similar to quarterbacks and their signal codes on tape. It is not that he needs hidden cues, because, after all, experts are permitted to bring notes to the stand. However, few experts think in a systematic way about how they should prepare memory joggers. This concerned psychologist would benefit from putting a great deal of one-time work into outlining key aspects of the literature and his assessment methodology, aspects that are likely to come up repeatedly. He should have a template for noting down what he needs to know for any one trial, and he should bring notes with him to the stand on both general content and case-specific content in a readily accessible form.

Being a pocket man or woman on the witness stand has great appeal. Your answers flow effortlessly. Every question is anticipated or understood. You have a bounty of goodies that impress and persuade within the boundaries of who you are. Observers who do not know better attribute extraordinary abilities to you. Although ability is a piece of it, planning ahead, preparing, and making a major commitment to organization is more of it. For other witnesses it is more appealing to see themselves as imperial masters of narrative who need no notes.

The question, in part, is what suits you. How do you normally present information? I have a colleague who shows five dozen PowerPoint slides in every class she teaches. She does well with notes.

Many midpoints exist between pocket men and quarterbacks, between the memorizers and the note takers. Many people find some middle ground. For the persons who pride themselves on memory and organization, they are well off leaning toward pocket competence. For those who prefer written notes to aid their memory and testimony, they are best off leaning toward the quarterback technique of notes and codes.

THE MAXIM: *Tailor your preparation for testimony to build on your strengths and compensate for your weaknesses. Memorize what you can. For the gaps that exist in memory and organization, invest heavily in preparing written outlines and memory aids before going to court.*

Defining Moments

I HAD SOUGHT OUT PETER ELLIS in the hope that I could learn more about the nature of the cross-examination in his trial 9 years earlier. In what arguably had been the most notorious trial in the history of New Zealand, Peter Ellis had been convicted in 1993 of charges that he had abused children at the Christchurch Civic Child Centre, known locally as the Christchurch Civic Crèche. Like other trials alleging ritual abuse, more than one hundred allegations had been filed against Ellis as well as four women who worked at the Crèche. Most of the charges were dropped, as were all of them against the four women defendants, but openly homosexual Ellis was tried, convicted, imprisoned, and subsequently released after 7 years in prison. In her book about the case, Lynley Hood (2001) came down clearly and unequivocally on the side of Ellis' innocence, as did I in my own understanding of the case.

I may have contributed in a modest way to his conviction. Just before the trial began, a protective services worker who would later testify for the prosecution attended my workshop on testifying in court at the University of Canterbury. After the workshop, she sought me out and I offered advice on how to handle the questions she most feared.

It made no difference to Ellis when I told him this after his release. However, it does raise the issue of whether one should attend to one's values when training people to be better witnesses. My resolution then and now is that good knowledge belongs to everyone. If forensic workshop leaders were to investigate who is right or wrong, guilty or innocent, in cases in which the workshop participants are involved, leaders would have to mobilize teams of investigators, all with considerable precognitive powers, to assess who is truly guilty.

In Peter Ellis' own testimony at his trial, one sequence of questions and answers became the cornerstone of the jurors' judgment of Ellis' guilt. Hood (2001) reported the sequence this way. Mr. Stanaway was the prosecuting attorney.

> About half-an-hour into his two-hour cross-examination, Ellis appeared to stumble. At the time, and in his closing address, Stanaway presented that apparent stumble as evidence that Ellis was an unreliable witness. Because he was an authoritative and confident prosecutor, and Ellis was a nervous defendant, the jury probably believed him. Curiously, according to the court transcript, that apparent stumble was not a stumble at all. But in view of the importance attached to the episode by the prosecution, and by people who supported the prosecution, we need to examine it more closely.
>
> At the time, Stanaway was cross-examining Ellis on discrepancies between his evidence and the evidence of Ms Kapok.
>
> "How did you normally get from 404 Hereford Street— when living there—to the crèche?" Stanaway asked.

"I walked," said Ellis. He said the walk took about 20 minutes, and that children could probably walk the distance in the same time.

"It would be possible though, wouldn't it, to walk from the crèche to the Square, catch a bus to Hereford Street, disembark and walk to Hereford Street, within 20 minutes?"

"I wouldn't know on the bus timetables because I walked."

"Are you telling us you never took a bus from Hereford Street to the crèche or back?"

"The buses didn't run down Hereford Street, or if they did it was very infrequent, it was far easier for me to walk. If on a rainy day I caught a bus, I would have gone and got it from the Worcester Street stand."

"You are now saying, are you, on rainy days you did catch a bus?"

"Yes, perhaps I did. I certainly remember basically walking. Obviously if it was really pouring with rain I would catch a bus."

"Didn't you just say to us you always walked, never took a bus?" said Stanaway. In fact, Ellis had said nothing of the sort, but the Crown Solicitor seemed to know what he was talking about, so Ellis took him at his word.

"Yes, I did say that. I'm sorry."

In retrospect, it seems hard to believe that anyone could regard that exchange as a defining moment in the trial. Nonetheless, to the prosecution, and to people who supported the prosecution, it was as if the Crown Solicitor had vanquished his foe with one blow of his broadsword, and was now displaying his head on a stake to the assembled crowd. (Hood, 2001, pp. 511–512)

When I asked Peter Ellis about this critical sequence, he had not thought about it much. Instead, he was more interested in ruminating about the whole process and his continuing efforts to be cleared of charges through legal or administrative channels.

Indeed, witnesses are often not the best resources for getting perspective on their own testimony. One plaintiff told me how her case was apparently lost because she disregarded her attorney's advice on how to answer questions, and ineffectively pursued her own understanding of how the civil charges should be understood and evaluated.

It is too late now for Peter Ellis to retract the simple statement that contaminated the perceived truthfulness of everything else he said. However, his key statement may serve us as a teaching lesson. He stated, "Yes, I did say that. I'm sorry."

The "I'm sorry" phrase weakened his credibility. It made it appear he was apologizing for being deceptive. The "Yes, I did say that" phrase came across as an explicit acknowledgment of a falsehood. What should he have said? "No. You are trying to put words in my mouth. That is not what I said. I did not say I never took the bus."

Peter Ellis did not tell me that he felt controlled and powerless at the time of this sequence. Ellis had other things that concerned him. But for other witnesses, when you feel as if your testimony is out of control and a cross-examining attorney has led you to the point of admitting inaccurate conclusions, think through the questions, listen with care, and answer with exactly what you wish to say.

THE MAXIM: *Credibility of testimony occasionally can revolve around brief questions and answers. Treat all of your testimony, even short and apparently insignificant answers, as important enough to think through and answer with care.*

Trivial Revenge

S OME OF WHAT GOES ON IN TESTIFYING in court is obvious and straightforward. You are asked questions, you answer them, and the business of the testimony gets completed. However, opposing attorneys, and every now and then retaining attorneys, sometimes act in petty ways that serve to disrupt your comfort or serenity—although for many witnesses the words *testifying* and *serenity* never occur in the same thought. Consider this example. The testimony had gone well. During the cross, the attorney had repeatedly tried to put words in my mouth. She kept asking questions that began with the phrase, "Surely, Doctor." Thus, she asked,

Q. Surely, Doctor, you would not deny that the defendant has a disorder that has been with him for at least 15 years right up to the present time?

A. I would surely disagree with your suggestion that the defendant was seriously disordered at the time I evaluated him.

Note the use of the word *surely* in the answer to emphasize that I was aware that her use of the word "surely" was
an effort to put words in my mouth. The repetition of "surely"
was a signal that I would be a player within the same linguistic
frame of reference. Before long, the word *absolutely* assumed
the place of prominence in her cross-examination.

Q. Isn't it *absolutely* true that symptoms never appear unexpectedly and briefly?
A. No, you are missing the essential point that I have made
   in my conclusions from my evaluation of Mr. Johnson. It
   is not only not *absolutely* true, it is not even *substantially*
   true in any sense.

Again, the answer sought to stay with the language used
in the question. Jurors like witnesses who appear to be on
target in replying to questions.

This attorney next waved in front of me an audiotape
made of the defendant speaking with his wife during a visit
in the jail. She told me what was in it, and asked if I was
familiar with the contents. I said I was not. She asked
incredulously if the attorneys who had retained me had not
told me about it or played it for me. "Nope. They did not
tell me about it. Neither did they play it for me," was
my answer.

The attorney was peeved. The next part of her cross-
examination consisted of her descriptions of what was in the
tape and asking me about whether it would affect my opinion.
Because the questions were never put forth as hypothetical
questions, my responses were all along the following lines:
"I have not had the chance to listen to the tape myself to
form any conclusions. I have no basis for opinions about the
conversations in the tape."

If the attorney had indeed asked me if it was hypotheti-
cally possible that certain thoughts and schemes were being

concocted, I would have been obliged to try to answer. Still, I could have replied that I did not have enough information to develop a hypothetical opinion.

After an hour of this back and forth questioning, the attorney was restless and unhappy that her planned cross had not been productive, and she concluded abruptly. A brief redirect followed, and there was no re-cross-examination. The judge was excusing me when this attorney asked that the judge order me to wait until the next witness, the only other mental health expert, finished testifying, in the event that she wanted to recall me to the stand.

This request came not from a serious intent to recall me to the stand. She knew she was not going to get what she had hoped for from my testimony. However, it was a request that fell in the category of what I have come to think of as trivial revenge.

The attorney and the judge both knew that I had driven 4 hours early in the morning that day to get to the courthouse, and that I was going back after my testimony. During a break the judge had asked which route I had taken: The longer but faster interstate trip or the more direct narrow road that is jammed with logging trucks and school buses? After my testimony I was weary and ready to get on the road. My chronic get-there-itis had set in. "Judge, it would be really helpful if I could leave now. I have a long trip back."

"Doctor, wait right outside the courtroom in case we need you," he ordered, "and you may step down."

"Yes, your honor."

The next witness was a professional acquaintance and we had discussed some aspects of the case. She had a lot to say and I knew she would be on the stand for hours. Still, the judge had ordered me to wait outside the courtroom. For the first 30 minutes of the next witness' testimony, I shifted around on the hard wooden bench in the corridor outside the courtroom, now and then peering through the window in the court-room door to see what was happening. I finally left the courthouse.

The small city in which this trial took place has a central square, with the courthouse in the center, and water fountains and park benches scattered around it. The spring day was mild and warm. I hung my jacket on the back of the bench, rolled up my sleeves, plugged the cell phone earpiece in place, microphone clipped to my shirt, and relaxed. I checked my phone messages and returned calls. I watched the finches, cardinals, and doves feeding close by. After a little while, the aggravation of having to stay passed. I went back to the courthouse and peered in again. The other expert was still testifying. A juror from another case stopped by and chatted. The reporter for the local newspaper sat with me, offered his opinions about what had gone on and explained to me what he thought about the case. The examination of the other expert witness eventually concluded, and the attorneys came out to tell me I would not be needed.

This keeping me on site fell within legitimate proce-dures used to annoy witnesses in trials. There are many other small intrusions that attorneys can use to irritate you. Sometimes they demand documents you do not have. Sometimes they insist you put your social security number, home address, yearly income, or kind of automobile you drive on record for the court. Other times they reschedule witnesses to delay or speed up your anticipated time of testimony.

Some attorney nonverbal postures serve the same pur-pose and are designed to make you feel diminished. These trivial revenges work if you allow them to work. If you can avoid taking them personally and avoid emotional reactivity and irritation, then you will have made progress to having mastered the situation.

THE MAXIM: *Attorneys may use trivial revenges when you have done well. Reconstruct them as signs of your success and adapt with your own best means of relaxation and comfort.*

❦ 22 ❦

Lies

DO EXPERTS ACTUALLY LIE ON THE STAND? In a different context, Ian M. Banks (2000) wrote:

> Oh, they never lie. They dissemble, evade, prevaricate, confound, confuse, distract, obscure, subtly misrepresent and willfully misunderstand with what appears to be a positively gleeful relish and are generally perfectly capable of contriving to give one an utterly unambiguous impression of their future course of action while in fact intending to do exactly the opposite, but they never lie. Perish the thought. (p. 23).

The well-known expert was being questioned during the direct examination. After going through his extensive

---

This chapter was part of a paper titled, "The Forensic Self," presented at the annual meeting of the American Psychological Association, San Francisco, August 26, 2001.

103

credentials, the famous man was asked about his academic affiliations. He stated that he was on the faculty of medicine of the nearby state university, when, in fact, he had only been invited to give a lecture to that university. In another trial the same famous expert was asked if he could, with a reasonable degree of medical certainty, draw conclusions about the personality, pathology, and dangerousness of the defendant with whom his only contact was observation of the accused sitting at the defense table. Most experts would respond that it was both impossible and unethical to draw such conclusions. He said he could, and did.

But why would this distinguished psychiatrist lie so? As background, let us note that he was flamboyant, unpredictable, and unconventional in many aspects of his life. When he testified in court, he offered an energetic and convincing style of presentation. A compelling witness, he was clear, absolutely confident, and always a teacher and a showman. At times his need to be a compelling and credible witness took priority over professional accountability. But why did he slide onto the shaky ground in the two instances noted?

Part of the answer was personal. He and I once attended together a showing of a documentary exposé of a psychiatric hospital. This expert himself figured prominently in one scene of the film in which he showed no empathy to a distressed patient. After the film, when introduced to the audience, he stood and waived obliviously and with pleasure to a round of vigorous boos and hisses. One could attribute his lack of professionally sound testimony to the same traits that led him to shatter windows, eat other persons' cold leftovers at restaurant tables, and not be bothered by the disapproval at the documentary showing. However, such explanations are trait-oriented and are overly easy explanations, in the sense that they lead us to rule out such behaviors as "not us." As we look at two other examples, state and situational demands will be presented as alternatives.

A second case observation came to me about a PhD psychologist who had testified in a sentencing hearing. The expert witness testified that the defendant would be less likely to reoffend if he was maintained on medications. The prosecuting attorney cross-examined the expert by asking if he had any training as a forensic psychologist. This psychologist responded that I had supervised some of his work and I was the "number two" forensic psychologist in the country.

In fact, this psychologist had graduated from our university's PhD program in clinical psychology, but he never took forensic or psychotherapy practicum, supervision, or research with me of any sort. As to his claim about my standing in forensic psychology, I am still waiting for the MTV review of greatest forensic hits to see if I can edge up into the top 50.

The third instance is a similar but milder example of misstating training credentials. As part of reviewing transcripts in capital trials, I read the transcribed testimony of an expert who completed his PhD with our university. In response to credentialing questions, he asserted that he had a PhD in "clinical and forensic psychology." Although this individual did indeed have a specialization in psychology-law, did take courses in forensic psychology, and did indeed have several years of experience as a psychologist in a forensic setting, he did not receive a PhD in clinical and forensic psychology. The university does not offer one.

Why did he say that he had? I can speculate that he was accustomed to thinking of himself in these terms. Perhaps he saw the report of his credentials as descriptive of content rather than a literal report and put it in these terms to make his degree more meaningful to the court.

In his testimony he stated that he spent between 1 and 2 hours interviewing the defendant for a mitigation assessment, and that the time included an unspecified psychological test. As a matter of routine practice, experts should be prepared to report exactly how much time they spent with a defendant, to indicate what testing was conducted, and to tailor an assessment to the task. It is fair to say that 1 to 2 hours is almost always insufficient for a task as broad and demanding as a mitigation evaluation.

The fourth instance was a person in a testifying workshop who reported lying while on the witness stand. During a discussion of tactics to use when confronted with challenging cross-examinations, this participant, who had testified as a treating expert, offered the statement, "Well, I lie." The entire group of workshop participants became quiet and focused. I asked if he could explain. He amiably proceeded to report how he had denied in court that he had ever been dismissed from a job, when in fact he had been dismissed (but was certain it would never be uncovered). He also reported that he had testified on another occasion that the materials that he had given opposing counsel during discovery were complete, when, in fact, he had withheld the tape recording of the interview. I gave him feedback about legal and ethical obligations while testifying.

The temptation with the four instances of testimony of these experts is to look toward character as exclusive explanations. That is, one can think of these persons as marginally ethical, as liars and deceivers, as persons willing to offer false testimony to come out ahead in the ordinary exchanges between expert witness and cross-examining attorney. There may occasionally be good character explanations. However, such explanations seem to be limited and problematic. Many thoroughly knowledgeable, ethical, and responsible experts who have conducted themselves well in most testimony do sometimes make incorrect statements. If confronted by a colleague, the individuals I have discussed would probably retract what they have said, as they should. But why would they say such things to begin with?

One explanatory framework is a state model of witness behavior, in which a transient testifying self sometimes dominates, in which overstatement and falsehoods are created to fit into the operating schema of the testifying self. Greenberg and Shuman (1997) have thoughtfully differentiated clinical–therapeutic roles from forensic roles on ten dimensions. Following their conceptualization, the following dimensions may help to distinguish state aspects of testifying and forensic roles. On each dimension noted in Table 22.1, role demands and behaviors are identified for experts in their typical forensic assessment or testifying roles. Enough wide variation exists between experts that only typical roles are addressed. Five dimensions are discussed: general methodology, self-disclosure, control, pull to fudge, and impartiality.

In dimension 1, general methodology, a moderate degree of standardization is present, at least among forensic institutions and among individual practices. In a 1999 survey (Boccaccini & Brodsky, 1999) a few tests were used repeatedly in civil forensic assessments. Indeed, one can see considerable standardization in the procedures associated with document review, interviews of third parties, and forensic interviews of plaintiffs or defendants. In contrast, standardization of testimony is primarily driven by the structure of courtroom procedures. Testifying experts approach manner of presentation, testimony style, and substance in highly variable ways. This

Table 22.1. Assessment Versus Testifying Roles

Dimension	Forensic assessment	Testifying
1. General methodology	Standardized	Variable
2. Self-disclosure	Minimal	May be extensive
3. Control	Extensive	Locus of control may be elsewhere
4. Pull to "fudge"	Infrequent	Not unusual
5. Attainment of impartiality	Practiced	Requires discipline

variability is never more apparent than when one watches many experts testifying in trials in which much is at stake. Often no two experts approach the presentation of their findings and conclusions in even close to the same manner.

A compelling difference is present on dimension 2, self-disclosure. In their evaluator roles, experts are consistently and impressively good at minimizing personal or professional disclosures. Adept at eliciting content from the subject, they stay tight-lipped about themselves. In contrast, the nature of credentialing, questions about experience, and the witness's common desire to impress often leads to extensive professional and moderate personal self-disclosure. Of course, it is proper to conceal self during assessments and selectively reveal self during testimony.

Control (dimension 3) shows major differences. While conducting assessments, our sense of being in control comes from this event being in our arena, with our issues, our methods, and our conclusions. In court, the locus of control is often but not always elsewhere. Experts do not know what they will be asked during cross (and sometimes during direct), and major elements of control rest in the decisions and strategies of attorneys and the court.

The pull to fudge (dimension 4) is always present in forensic work, often in the form of efforts by retaining attorneys to elicit a particular finding; less frequently, it appears on the part of assessors to come up with findings that shade toward the side that has retained them. How much this occurs is arguable. Margaret Hagen (1997) takes the position that it occurs often. I hold that it occurs occasionally. Conversely, the case examples I have given earlier in this chapter illustrate how readily the perceived or real attack during cross-examinations (and depositions) can lead toward fudging or edging of factual information, as well as shading of forensic findings.

The pull to fudge is inversely related to the last of the dimensions, the attainment of impartiality (5). This dimension may be thought of as the integrated whole of assessment and testimony roles. The standardization and training do help the assessor stay impartial. Impartiality is more difficult in court because of the immersion in the adversarial process.

The examples that were offered in this chapter were discovered opportunistically, without any intent to investigate. I suspect these are common misstatements and are reflections of the compromises that experts sometimes make in their testifying roles.

How to deal with it? First, we should heighten our awareness of the phenomenon. I have begun by sending copies of this chapter to the offending experts. Second, we should study it, in part by reviewing and assessing the material presented in court in credentialing of experts. Finally, we should engage in primary prevention by alerting graduate students and trial attorneys alike about the ethical slippage in such statements.

THE MAXIM: *Never assume that you are beyond the reach of situational pulls that may distort your testimony. Stay alert to and resist the courtroom pulls to overstate credentials and findings. When possible, review transcripts of your own testimony as a check of your accuracy.*

CROSS-EXAMINATION ATTACKS
AND BULLYING

❧ 23 ❧

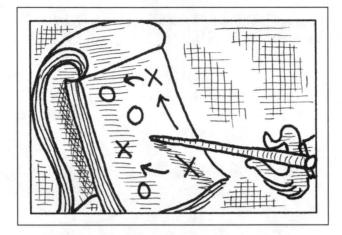

Anticipate Tactics of the Adversarial Attorney

IN HIS CLASSIC TEXT, *The Art of Cross-Examination,* Francis Wellman (1936/1997) wrote of the attorney conducting the cross-examination:

> It requires the greatest ingenuity; a habit of logical thought; clearness of perception in general; infinite patience and self-control; . . . ability to act with force and precision; a masterful knowledge of the subject-matter itself; an extreme caution. . . . It involves all shades and complexions of human morals, human passions, and human intelligence. (p. 28)

Consistent with the spirit of his times,[10] Wellman engages in great hyperbole. Let us begin with his phrase "the greatest ingenuity," and apply it to witnesses as well. It may not take the greatest ingenuity to be a great witness: after all, greatest compared to what or whom? Nevertheless, the other traits from his list do apply to witnesses, who, at their best, are indeed logical, patient, and perceptive when cross-examined. Part of being perceptive is to be aware of the tactics being used by the attorney.

Attorneys who shout or intimidate typically seek to discredit the witness rather than the testimony. Attempts to discredit the testimony, itself, however, often begin with a long, slow, soft pitch in which the attorney is courteous and conciliatory so that ". . .the witness will soon lose the fear that all witnesses have of the cross-examiner" (Wellman, 1936/1997, p. 30).

Attorneys and witnesses alike aspire to being extraordinary in their respective competing roles. Only a few succeed. A more realistic goal is to aspire to being effective, to understand their tasks and the demands on them, and to approach their tasks in a clear and knowledgeable manner. Attorneys and witnesses are alike in one more respect. Both can be harshly judgmental of their performances during cross. Attorneys often second-guess themselves and obsess about what they should have done. Sometimes they seek debriefings from colleagues about how well they did. Witnesses, too, often rethink the answers they gave, and in the hindsight that infuses them as they walk away from the courthouse, think of what should have been said, or how poorly they phrased an answer. Much as opposing sides in times of war demonize each other, so do many experts demonize the attorneys who have

---

[10] The first edition of this book was published in 1903.

conducted a successful cross. Yet, the questioning is more often predictable than demonic.

The cross-examination techniques advised by Wellman occur in the context of case examples and include an approach that might be titled "chastising the witness." Wellman wrote:

> The cross-examination of this witness is recorded here as an instructive example of the power of this legal weapon when in the hands of a master of the art even against an expert witness of such international prestige and highly specialized training in court proceedings as Dr. Jelliffe. (p. 401)

> Dr. Jelliffe was asked early in the cross:

> Q. . . . I would like you, because it is important, to search your memory for what was said. Is your memory normal? I think we will agree it is. Isn't it?"
> A. I don't know. That is for you to decide.
> Q. Very good. Now . . . .
> [The questions then go into the issues in the case.] (p. 401)

At this point, the witness has become suspicious. He has given an acceptable if disingenuous answer—after all, most of us know whether our memories are normal. The attorney then said "very good," setting up an apparent pattern of critical judgment of answers. This pattern continued when the witness answered the question of whether he observed repetition of ideas in the defendant. "Yes, he did that quite frequently." The attorney then admonished him. "Now, doctor, when I ask you a question, will you please stick to the question I ask you and not go off to something else?"

Once again, the witness is chastised. The questioning continues:

> Q. Didn't you attempt to bring his mind to specific things in connection with it, in the face of his denial?

A. I think I have already testified to that, yes.
Q. Never mind to what you have already testified
to; I want to know what you did.
A. I think I have already told you. (p. 405)

In chapter 10 I discussed how personal references and the phrase "I think" diminish the power of a reply. Thus, what reply to "I want to know what you did" would put the witness in a position of strength? Here are three categories of possible answers: simple, reflective, and method-oriented answers.

The simple answer:

A. Yes, of course.

The reflective answer:

A. No matter how many different ways you rephrase your question, my answer remains, yes, that I confronted and assessed the defendant when he was in denial.

The method-oriented answer:

A. Confront, no: assess, yes.

This last answer has much implied but not stated. Most attorneys would follow with an open-ended question that allows the witness to develop a full narrative answer.

In the same cross, the witness testified that the defendant had told distinctly inappropriate off-color stories during the mental health examination.

Q. Well, a lot of normal people do inappropriate things, don't they, without affecting their mental worth or ability?
A. I think a great many people that pass for normal do just that sort of thing.

Here the witness was defensive. He would have been better off simply saying, "Certainly, normal people do inappropriate things, some as a result of mental problems." Note Dr. Jelliffe's use of the phrases "a great many people" and "pass for normal." The witness could have said "many people" and avoided the sense of exaggeration. More convincing would have been the omission of the pass-for-normal phrase altogether. He took the unnecessary step of expanding the nature of the issue from normal people to apparently normal people. The real answer, if one thinks about it, is that inappropriate behaviors belong to everyone and may be seen in just about everyone at selective times.

It may seem as if this discussion dwells on minor points and on small issues. However, cross-examinations are mostly made up of just such small points, which either build or take apart the content of the direct.

A reciprocal attribution of power often exists between cross-examining attorneys and expert witnesses. Attorneys are taught in school and workshops that much of the power rests within the specialized knowledge of experts and the task in the cross is to ask only questions to which the answer is known. Experts, in turn, fear the cross as a time at which tricky or ingenious attorneys twist ideas and elicit lack of knowledge. In fact, both perspectives are partly true. Witnesses can learn from what attorneys fear, including the consequences of the unnecessary cross or overdoing the cross (Wellman, 1936/1997, p. 205).

The unnecessary cross takes place when the testimony during direct has made few useful points, but the opposing attorney wants to make more of the situation. One case example: Little personal information about a defendant that would be harmful to the prosecution had come out in direct. During the cross-examination, an ill-considered question allowed the witness to say of the defendant, "he is a very fine family man, he is a good father to his children, he is a good husband to his wife, (and) he lives in a very noble way in his neighborhood" (p. 207).

Neither typical attorneys nor typical witnesses are skilled at understanding the cross-examination through the eyes of their counterparts. It is rare to find an expert witness who reads material about what is told to attorneys about cross. It is not as rare but still not common for attorneys to study about what is taught to expert witnesses. A good knowledge of the other is a major constructive step in mastering the challenging cross-examination.

THE MAXIM: *Attorneys may chastise or corner witnesses during cross-examinations. Good witnesses stay effective and in control through simple, reflective, or method-oriented answers that come out of purposeful knowledge of attorney techniques.*

✤ 24 ✤

Bullying Attorneys

THE PROBLEM OF BULLYING IN ELEMENTARY AND HIGH SCHOOLS is widespread and harmful. The customary definition of bullying is a form of aggression in which the bully has more power than the victim, and in which social dominance is imposed on a person who has a visible vulnerability. Most people have stories to tell about being victims of bullying or themselves having been bullies. My own painful memories of being bullied include two older, larger youths walking behind me in seventh grade school corridors and stepping on my heels as part of shaking me down for my lunch money. To this day, when somebody accidentally steps on my heels, it produces a visceral anxious reaction.

These constructs about bullying and victimization were drawn in large part from presentations and related publications by Wendy Craig of Queens University, Kingston, Ontario, Canada.

Bullying hardly stops in the school system. In adult personal relationships, bullying may be thought of as abuse. In workplaces, bullying is relabeled as harassment. In medical settings, bullying may be seen as part of top-down organizational intrusions and insensitivity. In competitive athletic settings, bullying is much like it is in the schools—widespread, one-sided picking on a weaker or vulnerable person that is supported by colleagues. When we speak of aggression in which the bully has more power than the victim, we should emphasize that such power is acquired particularly through social dominance and through knowing the vulnerability of likely victims.

Bullying and victimization exist in the courtroom, as well. It is beyond my reach to address the concept of judges as occasional bullies, but attorneys' behaviors are clearer. When witnesses are testifying on the stand, three dynamics of attorney bullying can be present:

1. Power imbalance, with witnesses and attorneys alike perceiving that attorneys have more power.

2. The bully's intent to harm, in this case to harm personal and professional credibility and worth.

3. Subsequent victim distress, in the form of stumbling, tense, or weak behaviors.

Considerable data support the assertion that bullying is common. In one study, psychologist Wendy Craig and her colleagues asked 2,356 boys and 2,366 girls if they had been bullied in the last 5 days. One half to two thirds of the youths reported that they had been bullies or bullied (Craig, Pepler, & Atlas, 2000). When cordless microphones were put on kids in playgrounds to monitor their behaviors, no differences were found between boys and girls but girls reported being bullies much less than did boys. So, too, it is in court—women attorneys are less likely to see themselves as bullies when they are highly assertive in questioning witnesses.

When attorneys have good cognitive and verbal skills, their bullying takes on sophisticated forms. It is a reasonable extrapolation of research knowledge to assume that attorneys' verbal aggression in depositions and cross-examinations has developed over their life span. Starting in elementary school or earlier, they become increasingly aggressive. Bullies often have themselves been victims of bullying, and bullying becomes a means for them to cope with anxiety and other internalized problems (Craig & Pepler, 1997; Rahey & Craig, 2002). Because teen bullies are notably more likely than their peers to use alcohol and drugs, substance abuse may be present for adults, including attorney bullies. It may be related to marital and child abuse, too. Attorney bullying does not always represent good questioning or knowledgeable inquiries. Indeed, the best questions and most effective cross-examinations are often pursued respectfully. Rather, attorney bullying of witnesses involves process, not content, in which intimidation, a demeaning manner, and nasty or abrasive questioning are used.

Generalizing about victimization to witnesses is more difficult because of powerful courtroom contextual and situational factors. Elementary school students who were regularly victimized had anxiety and somatic symptoms and tended to be withdrawn. Girls often had eating disorders. I have spoken to many lay witnesses and experts who report consistent harassment on the stand, so that they clearly feel victimized. The following excerpt describes a 14-year-old girl who was giving evidence in an Australia sexual abuse hearing involving her father; it illustrates bullying of a witness:

> When the time came for her to be questioned by the defence barrister, she was ill-prepared for the hours to come. She was almost immediately reduced to tears, and cried for the duration as the defence barrister grilled her—frequently shouting and thumping his fist on the bar table. . . . She

was asked by the defence more than 30 times to describe her father's penis. How long was it? How wide was it? What did the 'end' of it look like? She was asked to draw the penis "to scale." Her attempts were scrutinized over and over, despite her protestations that she could not draw very well. Fifteen times the magistrate intervened in the cross-examination, warning the lawyer to keep his voice down, and that there was to be no "badgering" or "harassing" of the witness. The magistrate even threatened to call a halt to the proceedings and send the matter straight for trial. But . . . the defence barrister was unrepentant and the abuse of Chrissie in society's halls of justice continued. (Wenham, 2002, p. 27. See also Eastwood, 2002.)

Chrissie was like other persons who have been bullied and victimized on the stand, because they carry an element of vulnerability. Some expert witnesses have had several similar—but less severe—experiences. A person probably has an accessible and visible vulnerability if he or she is victimized severely, often, and for much of the time when testifying. Generalizing from other spheres of knowledge, people at risk for victimization tend to be anxious, to blush, and to get embarrassed easily. They have patterns of social withdrawal. Their parents may have been protective; the victims often have high warmth and intimacy in their lives, but they also feel alienated.

In the schoolyard when a fight breaks out, kids come to watch. Then the aggression increases. Behavior becomes escalated. The same thing happens when the bullying gets the rapt attention of the courtroom. An escalation in intensity of the cross-examination may occur as the drama of commanding the stage and audience supports the bullying. It is emotionally arousing to the attorney and sufficiently exciting to the audience that courthouse workers may come to watch.

Feedback from the attorney's peers can sometimes shape these behaviors. In one sexual harassment case in which I was an observer, one attorney sought out the bullying opposing counsel, and gently gave him feedback that such behaviors were out of line. Continuing legal education should also address these behaviors, although I know of no instance in which such education has done so.

What should you do if confronted with a bullying attorney while you are testifying? Some witnesses try to be equally aggressive and every loud or insulting question is met in kind. These responses tend not to work. The witness's credibility and impartiality are compromised.

One way of handling attorney bullying is through presentation of self in the opposite way. If the attorney asks loud and insistent questions, respond with quiet, assured, measured responses. If the attorney demands an immediate and unreasonable answer, reply with a careful, thought-out, reasonable reply. Do not be captured by the aggressive style of the questions. Take time to think and answer in ways that are consistent with who you are and how you think of the issues. Draw on your already known strengths for handling crises and apply them on the stand.

THE MAXIM: *Like all bullies, bullying attorneys look for vulnerabilities and depend on witnesses to be intimidated. Handle bullying questions by practicing and mastering interpersonal strength and professional poise under fire.*

❧ 25 ❧

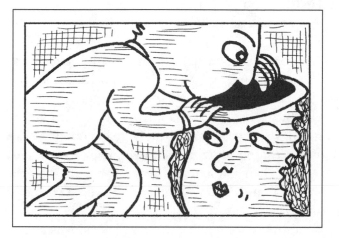

Involuntary Disclosure of Forensic Self

I N COURT, ATTORNEYS SOMETIMES ASK FOR or demand access to one's personal and professional life. Unlike "the private sharing of professional self" (Brodsky, 1993) in which experts disclose forensic content with family and friends, these queries seek forensic sharing of private self.

This involuntary sharing of one's work or life arises when witnesses have a private or embarrassing issue brought to light during a legal proceeding. Such private events are elicited in depositions, in particular, but also in trial testimony. The witnesses may be confronted with accurate, distorted, or untrue characterizations of something they have done.

One witness was asked the following three unexpected questions in a deposition:

Q1. Isn't it true the police have been called to your house because of domestic abuse?

Q2. Isn't it true you have been a party in a physical abuse of a child?

123

Q3.   Isn't it true that you have had an evaluation for drug and alcohol abuse?

The first question had no truth to it whatsoever. The expert was infuriated by the question, fumed, denied the allegation, and obsessed about it for weeks afterward. He was so distressed by the implied allegation that he was leaning toward bringing an ethical complaint to the state bar or filing a defamation suit against the attorney. However, litigants get little satisfaction from such lawsuits. A better focus may be how to handle questions of this sort that have such pejorative suggestions.

A desirable approach is a controlled calm, accompanied by a simple denial. For example, the indignant expert might have said: "These false suggestions are insulting and offensive to me. I do not know what the law and bar allow, but that kind of accusation is profoundly offensive." Such a response would serve as a sharp slap on the hand.

The second question had an element of truth in it. This expert had been himself severely abused as a child, although he had thought that minimal public records existed about this abuse. He found this a sensitive topic. His literal answer could have been, yes, he had been a party in the sense of having been a victim of abuse. However, he did not want others to know about these elements in his childhood that he felt were personal and shameful. This witness handled it well. He answered that it was not at all true that he had ever abused any child or adult in any situation.

The final question called for a literal yes answer. When he was 17, the expert had been arrested for possession of marijuana. Because as an adult professional he had applied for a position for which security clearance was needed, he had written about this arrest on the application. The agency to which he applied had a routine drug and alcohol abuse evaluation conducted for all applicants who indicated any relevant history. The subsequent evaluation resulted in a report of no problems with substance abuse.

The difficulty was that the expert did not want his application to the agency nor his required evaluation to be a matter of public record. Indeed, he was puzzled how the confidential information came to be accessible to the attorney. His reactions were to declare that he would not be insulted in this way and that the deposition was over, and to storm out of the building. This kind of behavior leads to a perception of guilt and unprofessionalism. If one commits oneself to forensic work, one should expect occasional hostile and personally probing questions.

What should he have done? He should have answered succinctly and objectively. "Yes," he should have said, "I was arrested for possession of marijuana at 17, but I do not have a drug or alcohol problem. The evaluation was part of a routine requirement of an agency with which I have a working relationship and it showed no problem." This chapter has addressed the general problem of intrusive questions. The next chapter examines gendered intrusions.

THE MAXIM: *Do not become ruffled when sensitive personal questions are asked, but rather stay controlled, factual, and nondefensive. Consider looking into possible ethical violations by the attorney as an absolute last resort.*

Gendered Invasion of Witness Privacy

PARTICIPANTS IN MY WORKSHOPS often share tales of how their personal privacy has been sacrificed. Although invasions into witness privacy take many forms, one of the most common is intrusion into highly personal experiences of women witnesses. In a Texas workshop, one after another intrusive questions were described by women experts, with other women subsequently affirming that they had been asked similar questions. Here are the categories of questions and specific questions they had been asked, almost always in the context of family court hearings or personal injury depositions.

Pregnancy and childbirth inquiries:

- Have you ever miscarried?
- Have you ever had an abortion?
- At exactly what point in your pregnancy did you have the miscarriage/abortion?
- Have you given birth?
- Do you have children? If no, Why not?

Familial inquiries (the first three questions were asked during a disputed custody hearing in which infidelity was an issue):

- To your knowledge, has your husband ever cheated on you?
- Have you ever cheated on your husband?
- Isn't it true that you are advocating custody for this father because you would like to have an affair with him?
- What side of the bed do you sleep on?
- Who else lives in your house with you? What are their names? What do they do for a living?
- What forms of discipline do you use with your children? How often?
- Have you ever been divorced? How many times?

Victimization inquiries (asked in cases in which a party or child is alleged to have been abused or raped):

- Have you ever been sexually abused?
- Have you ever been physically abused?
- Have you ever been raped?
- Have you ever been coerced into any unwanted sexual contact?

Substance use inquiries:

- What medications are you on now?
- What medications have you ever been on?
- For what specific medical purposes or personal problems?
- What kinds of alcoholic beverages do you drink? How often? How much?
- What illegal drugs have you ever used? How much? For how long?

Miscellaneous intrusive inquiries:

- Are you personally familiar with symptoms of PMS?
- Have you ever been arrested or charged for any offense? Identify each in chronological order.
- Isn't it true, doctor, that you are merely a defense whore?
- Have you ever seen an X-rated video?

The offensive intrusions went beyond these illustrative examples. When these women testifying on the stand or in depositions tried to demur, they were ordered by the court or attorneys to answer the questions. The male expert witnesses in the workshop had never been asked such questions in many years of testifying in court. One of the men explained that he never even gave his home address when asked, but only his business address. "It is a matter of privacy I feel strongly about." He had never been required to give his home address.

These were not isolated and idiosyncratic small towns in which the questions were asked but in good-sized cities. I offer two suggestions for replying to these intrusive questions.

1. Tell all such attorneys that these are personal and private matters that you discuss only with valued family members and trusted friends. When the questions are repeated, state again with emphasis that these are private matters, and discussed only with trusted friends.

2. Answer that the information presented during the testimony and the related professional judgments were based only on standardized, accepted, professional methods used accordingly with your training, skills, experience, and background. The testimony was not based in any way on personal issues, as implied in the intrusive questions, which might affect ordinary lay judgments.

Suppose both of these methods of responding fail. What next? If ordered to reply to such offensive questions, and if they choose to reply, women should keep their answers minimal in length and respond in a neutral manner. They should not overexplain why they are on any drug, psychotropic or not. Their manner should be sufficiently composed to communicate to the jurors and to the court that they are okay with their personal histories and choices. If the audience senses they are upset and defensive, the admissions will take on exaggerated meaning. If the court recognizes that the admissions are not distressing, the admissions will take on diminished meaning.

These women experienced harassing questions for a number of reasons specific to where they lived and practiced, but the gender issue is generalizable. Maureen O'Connor of John Jay College in New York has conducted research on intrusive questions directed at women and not men. O'Connor found that no male expert witnesses were asked such questions, an observation consistent with my reports from these and other cases. About one-fourth of the women witnesses at some time were asked such questions according to O'Connor's research (O'Connor & Mechanic, 2000).

These patterns are sexist in nature and reflect a gendered harassment of women witnesses. Such questions may sometimes be deflected. Two women in the Texas workshop had been unable to deflect the questions and it led them to dread going to court. These comments do not fully answer the question of why women and not men are asked such questions. After all, stating that it is sexism only describes the problem rather than answers the causal question.

The "whys" call for speculation, but here are some working hypotheses. The women are asked such questions because the cross-examining attorneys, men and women, assume they can get away with them. A milieu of tolerance for sexist intrusiveness exists in those courts and those cities. The questions are asked and allowed because there is a lack of professionalism in those courts. The questions are asked because the attorneys themselves operate with ongoing toxic gender assumptions about how women may be "properly" harassed.

Lastly, women who are asked gendered questions should set an early, clear, absolute boundary beyond which they will not answer questions. They should use the broken record method of repeating that these are personal, private, and unrelated to the scientific methods used. If the judge asks, respond, "Your honor, I wish I could be of help to the court, but these are questions that we psychologists never answer in court."

◉

THE MAXIM: *Gender-intrusive questions should be turned away with statements of privacy and clarification of the professional foundations of findings and testimony. If coerced to reply, keep answers minimal.*

◉

◉

❧ 27 ❧

Physical Threats

IT IS THE EMOTIONAL CIRCUMSTANCES of being criticized or attacked during cross-examination that most concerns witnesses. Aside from portrayals in overdramatized television shows, it is rare that witnesses ever feel genuinely concerned about physical harm. In child custody cases, experts have described out of court threats from the nonfavored parent. These threats have included stalking, threatening telephone calls, and angry letters with suggestions that the expert better "watch out." Yet, every now and then, cross-examining attorneys find a courtroom-acceptable interpersonal posture in which a physical threat is communicated in the guise of exploring an issue at hand. Consider the events that one psychologist described to me:

> I was testifying as an eyewitness expert in a case in which the perpetrator had gotten into the back seat of a man's car as the man was waiting in a parking lot. The perpetrator put a screwdriver to the man's neck and demanded his money. During

131

the trial the prosecutor walked over to me and put the screwdriver up to my neck (without actually touching it—that would have been even more outrageous) and asked me if I had ever had a screwdriver put up to my neck. I looked over to the defense attorney with this look of anguish; to my dismay, he did nothing. Afterwards, he told me that he wanted the jury to see "how much of an asshole" the prosecutor really was. I have no idea what verdict resulted. I do remember that it took me the entire 90 minute drive back to my house to calm down.

What should this witness have done? She did one thing exactly correctly. She waited for the attorney who had retained her to act. Given his inaction, three further possible courses of action stand out. First, and perhaps most preferable, she could have asked for the assistance of the judge. That is, she could have turned in her seat, looked directly at the judge, and said, "Your honor, counsel is holding a screwdriver to my neck."

In almost every instance, the judge would have become alerted to the inappropriateness of the action. The judge would then caution or order the attorney to step back and take the screwdriver away from the witness. This outcome is desirable in particular because the power and authority of the court has intervened.

A second option would be to confront the cross-examining attorney directly, by asserting strongly: "You are holding that screwdriver very close to my neck. Take it away now."

This response would have mobilized almost all parties in the courtroom. The bailiff would look to see if the witness was in danger. The retaining attorney would be up and involved. The judge might get active, too.

The third choice is to personally move the screwdriver to the side. This option may become clearer in another context.

One witness described what she did when an opposing attorney put his face perhaps 6 inches away from hers during questions. She waved her hand between them as if creating a breeze and said to the judge that the attorney has bad breath. "Could you ask him to stand back?" The attorney scurried back with considerable speed. Physically moving the screwdriver with an accompanying comment makes it evident that the screwdriver near her neck was a physical threat and was being treated as such.

THE MAXIM: *In the rare event that you feel physically threatened on the stand, do not passively accept it. Intervene actively to get the assistance of the judge or others.*

Ingratiation

INGRATIATION IS AN ORDINARY ASPECT of social interactions. People flatter and compliment others in order to achieve the goals of approval, liking, and favorable actions. Many ingratiating statements are part of long-term, well-established behaviors in which generalized acceptance and smooth transactions are the aim. In the southern United States, low-key flattery is the *lingua franca* of business and personal relationships. My next-door neighbor, who I know only in passing, tells me what a wonderful neighbor I am (which is not how I evaluate myself) and that she loves me (which is perhaps true in a broad understanding of agape).

In his book, *You're Too Kind: A Brief History of Flattery*, Richard Stengel (2000) opens with a vivid illustration of ingratiation, writing,

> Perfect, gentle reader, I will not begin this book
> with a tribute to your discernment, because a
> person of your obvious accomplishments would

certainly be immune to such blandishments. You would surely see through such transparent puffery and reject it out of hand. Someone with as much self-assurance and insight as you would not want any soft soap and sycophancy, but rather candor and direct truth. (p. 12)

According to Stengel, the classic model of the flatterer was Eddie Haskell from the 1960s television show *Leave It to Beaver*. Eddie Haskell was a smooth-talking kid perpetually ingratiating to adults, but who was an untrustworthy and manipulative weasel among his peers. Stengel offers a fourfold taxonomy of ingratiation. *Stroking* is insincere flattery designed to curry favor. *Sucking up* refers to a person of lower status acting to brownnose or bootlick a person of higher status for a definite payoff. *Edibles* are candied or honeyed words to flatter. Finally, *rhetoric* is an exaggerated or inflated statement designed to please.

In the courtroom, ingratiation takes on different meanings. When attorneys conduct a jury selection, they sometimes engage in flattery of the jury panel to a degree that borders on outrageous hyperbole. They tell jurors that the country is grateful to them for their unselfish service, and that the United States has the greatest legal system in the world because of their willingness to serve on juries. They praise the jurors in advance for their dedication, courage, and perceptiveness. At times when I listen to such statements, I feel as if I am drowning in insincerity, and briefly wonder if jurors could possibly believe such saccharine compliments. In a preliminary investigation into the effects of attorney ingratiation in jury selection, a student of mine, David Cannon (2001), has found that moderate levels of ingratiation in general, and flattery, in particular, lead to the most liking of attorneys.

In cross-examination during expert testimony or during depositions, ingratiating questions can take on a challenging or threatening quality. Attorneys might ask questions similar to the following:

Q1. You consider yourself a very careful observer of human behavior, don't you?

Q2. Do you think it is fair to say that you are the most knowledgeable forensic examiner in this entire county?

Q3. After all of the things you have done that you have described from your resume, would you agree that you have a very high level of expertise in your field?

Rather than these questions serving to flatter, they have the potential for bringing out apparent self-promotion and arrogance in witnesses who affirm the exaggeration. One should assume that the attorney has a follow-up question to challenge the level of admitted expertise, a question that has to do with national recognition, board certifications, or experience. If the expert agrees that she or he has a remarkable level of expertise, then the expert may have to defend such assertions. If the expert demurs, then the expertise may seem diminished.

One may respond by addressing the tactic. Thus, the expert might respond, "Such prideful and self-inflated statements are considered unbecoming in my field of professional work. My training and background that I testified about during the beginning of the direct examination accurately represent what I have done."

In any case, experts should avoid comparisons. In reality, almost no expert witnesses have been in a position to compare their knowledge to that of other professionals with precision, and that accurate humility should be stated.

The first question noted earlier, offers an interesting challenge. Should one agree that she or he is indeed a careful observer? Most witnesses probably should explain that they do observe others in a standardized and systematic manner by virtue of their training.

One of the consistent research findings about ingratiation is that it usually works, depending on the context (see, e.g., the seminal book on ingratiation by Edward E. Jones, 1964). Expert witnesses are often suspicious and uncomfortable when presented with queries about their high levels of knowledge, achievement, and skill, and, therefore, the ingratiation by attorneys may achieve the goal of putting the experts in an uncomfortable position. What should experts do? They should seek to respond with ease. They should feel free to state that they do not know, or that it should be others' conclusions if their achievements reach the threshold of being extraordinary or remarkable. Finally, they should try to maintain a quiet, unimposing, and centered self-confidence in replying to such questions.

THE MAXIM: *When ingratiating attorneys try to lead you to bragging and to statements of self-inflated attainments, stay with the facts of your credentials and dispel the flattery ploy with self-contained and unimposing assurance.*

III

EXPERTISE AND BASES
FOR TESTIMONY

PROFESSIONAL DILEMMAS
AND BOUNDARIES

✣ 29 ✣

Transcripts of Problem Depositions

JEFFREY POPKIN FOUND HIMSELF IN A DILEMMA. While working in his professional capacity as a forensic psychologist, he had given a 6-hour deposition as an expert for the defense in a civil case. The deposition was long, detailed, and contentious, and left Dr. Popkin with a problem. He described it in these terms.

> At one point in the deposition, the attorney for the plaintiff was able to get me to change my opinion on one important issue. He had succeeded by focusing on the language in one sentence in a set of somewhat ambiguous regulations. My original findings were based on the entire clause. I gave in. I agreed that I had been wrong in how I thought about the essential issues and what they meant for my findings. When I reread the section after the deposition I found my original findings to be correct.

142

> I will soon be receiving a copy of my deposi-
> tion to sign. I know that when I make the correc-
> tions to my deposition, this plaintiff's attorney
> may use the corrections and my original statement
> during the deposition to attack my credibility in
> court. Any suggestions on how I can handle
> this situation?

There is one overriding suggestion that cannot help Jeff Popkin at all. The principle is to prepare sufficiently that you know the law, including the psycholegal discussions and discourse in the literature about it. Once the law is well understood, then ensure that your findings and opinions follow logically, are sufficiently complete, and are double checked so that they are invulnerable (well, less vulnerable) to such attacks.

The degree of professional preparation for court and forensic work is greater than for nonforensic activities. The preparation needs to be comprehensive when professional assessment and legal rules coincide. Some professionals find that their workloads and fixed obligations do not permit such a comprehensive review. Nevertheless, such professionals should always make time anyway and think about comprehensive preparation as an ongoing and routine process. Persons who seek to prepare exhaustively at the last minute find it an unmanageable task. Persons who build in regular, systematic preparation in small units as part of everyday or weekly schedules find it manageable and productive.

For the kind of specific situation Dr. Popkin presented, a beginning point is to accept that deposition transcripts cannot be changed to correct substantive errors. It is tempting to correct poor thinking, flawed conclusions, and the fractured syntax of spoken language seen in written form. It is not okay to make such corrections when you review a deposition transcript. Reviewing depositions is only for the purposes of ensuring that the court reporter has been accurate—not that we witnesses have been accurate.

There are always times in which we say foolish and ill-phrased things to friends, to clients, and to colleagues. If we spend our time obsessing about what we should have said and the correct form and gist of it, most of us will hardly have time for living. I can retrieve from memory on demand many of my embarrassing and bumbling statements. But obsessing about these actions serves little purpose. Learning from it, well, that is another story.

What happens in court after one has said something incorrect or foolish in a deposition is an interesting question. Let us take the Popkin example. He should speak with the retaining attorney about the issue, to prepare the attorney for the question during trial, and to see if he needs to submit an addendum to his report. He should be prepared to state in court what happened, namely, that the question he answered in the deposition may have been misleading because of the language used. He should be clear that he did not intend then to change his opinion and does not now change his original opinion. He needs to be firm and explain possible confusion about the deposition answers.

<hr>

THE MAXIM: *Deposition transcripts may be corrected only if the court reporter was inaccurate, and not if the witness was inaccurate. Corrections in substance need to be discussed with counsel or await opportunities to elaborate during trial testimony.*

When Unprepared

AT THE END OF THE FILM, "As Good as It Gets," the character played by Jack Nicholson awkwardly kisses Helen Hunt for the first time. A pause follows. Then Nicholson says, "I know I can do much better than that."

That is how I felt after I had just testified about a defendant's psychological ability to enter into a plea bargain. The 2 days leading up to the testimony had been convoluted. The defendant had spent the previous 3 years in jail awaiting trial and protesting his innocence. A few days before the trial the prosecution, the defense attorneys, and this defendant had all agreed that he would enter a plea of guilty with a sentence of life without parole; in return, the death penalty was dropped as a possible sentence. When the attorney and defendant came to court for the required minitrial[11] for the case, I was down the hall in another courtroom.

The assistant to the lead attorney breathlessly burst through the doors, and ran to me. "You need to come right away," she gasped. Puzzled, I followed her down the hall in time to hear the defendant giving the judge a rambling and emotional denial that he had murdered anyone. He spoke about his innocence and how his attorneys had misled him. "I don't want to plead guilty," he declared in a whining voice. In the midst of his confused declaration, the defendant accurately stated that his friend involved in the murder had not been charged and now was scheduled to testify for the state.

Many conferences with attorneys and phone calls later that day, I learned that my associate who had tested the defendant was scheduled to be out of town the next day, the one full day of testimony in the minitrial. She had assessed the defendant for competence to stand trial, she knew him well, and the one and only day they needed her to testify, she had an unbreakable commitment elsewhere. As a result of hurried discussions and my exaggerated sense of professional responsibility, I found myself scheduled to testify with minimal preparation in court in her place the next day.

Moving like a dust devil, I looked quickly at the Godinez v. Moran (1993) Supreme Court decision, which held that the criteria for competency to stand trial applied equally to other related criminal competencies, such as competency to plea bargain. I skimmed other psychological–legal sources, such as the book by Melton, Petrila, Poythress, and Slobogin (1997). Before testifying, and between appointments of my own that

---

[11] The minitrial in Alabama is an abbreviated trial in which agreed facts in evidence are presented to a jury. Although the sentence is prearranged, a capital murder charge requires this token trial.

could not be rescheduled, I scoured the 3-inch-thick files of the defendant, unsuccessfully attempting to read my associate's handwriting, glancing at hospital, jail, and school records, taking notes on test results, and attempting to get an overall picture. I was the only witness called by the defense. I was not prepared. It was not how I like to be organized before testimony.

The questions were not difficult or unusual. I reported on IQ results. I described the defendant's adequate cognitive ability to appreciate the charges, proceedings, and outcomes. At the end of the direct examination the defense attorney knowingly asked: "Did you find a history of the defendant being abused when you looked at his social history records?" I had a vague idea that I had seen such information, but it was unclear and uncertain. I honestly replied: "I don't remember seeing such records."

She asked again, in different words, obviously hoping to get his abuse history in evidence. I gave the same answer again, trying to be matter-of-fact about it. My testimony did not last a long time. The cross-examination was mild and unremarkable. I was excused. But I was not happy. Instead of my normal sense of assuredness on the stand, I had felt tentative, and it showed. Instead of a mastery of the details and facts, I had a sketchy memory of this man's life, and that showed too.

It was not catastrophic. The results of the minitrial were exactly as they would have been without my testimony or if my associate had testified. I had answered the questions in a mostly satisfactory way. However, I set my standards for testifying higher than that. I lost the sense of weaving together the threads of the case and defendant into a smooth fabric of narrative and behaviors. Because I knew too little, I rushed. I could have done much better than that.

What should one do when called unexpectedly into court on short notice? Above all, stay faithful to your data. Do not extrapolate more than you should. If the opportunity arises, do not hesitate to tell the court that you have not prepared. Honest admissions of being called at the last minute and not having done everything you might have can be effective (and occasionally endearing), if you are okay with being honest this way. Above all, remember that the delivery is important. Even acknowledgments of insufficient preparation are acceptable when presented in a confident, comfortable way. Say that you wish you had been given more time to prepare, but say it in a manner that reflects a commitment to professionalism.

THE MAXIM: *One should make the best of being called to testify on short notice with little opportunity to prepare. Be honest, seek to be confident about the limitations of your knowledge, and allow your manner to transcend your uncertainties.*

❧ 31 ❧

Translations

T HIS WAS THE SECOND FULL DAY the psychiatrist had been in the witness stand. It was literally a witness stand, because in Australia witnesses stand while giving their testimony. We were in the Melbourne courtroom in which the most serious criminal trials are heard. The male judge with an earring stud sat robed in a bright red gown under a carved wood canopy, the barristers stood in their black robes and curled wigs, and the witness leaned against the round railing in an elevated small circular box as he spoke.

The defendant was an elderly Chinese woman. None of the essential facts were in dispute. Without provocation the defendant had repeatedly stabbed and eventually killed another woman in the nursing home that had been her latest placement after years of psychiatric hospitalization. Sitting next to the defendant in the third row of the public seating of the courtroom was one of her attorneys, who whispered a continuous translation into the defendant's ear.

The direct examination had been completed earlier. The psychiatrist had testified the defendant was competent to stand trial. A second psychiatrist yet to testify had submitted his report stating that she was not competent and he was watching and listening from the back of the courtroom. The 11 members of the jury sat in two elevated rows on the side of the room.

For hours, the cross-examination questions began with the same phrase: "Are you aware?" The content was similar, too. It always dealt with the defendant's substantial history of psychological disorders, hospitalizations, suicide attempts, and bizarre behaviors. Some were acknowledged; some were disputed. Then the issues of the translators and cultural context arose.

In each instance a translator had been used during the competency examinations. The barrister asked:

Q. How did you conclude that you had truly taken into account the cultural aspects of Cantonese Chinese culture?

A. If I may go into hearsay, your honor, I consulted with Professor Ling about the role of honor and face in Canton. I was informed that being seen as insane was much more unacceptable than being a criminal, and that such behaviors are hidden.

Q. So Mrs. Yu may have been hiding her illness?

A. When I spoke to Professor Ling, he discussed how such self-presentation and information appears.

At this point, the witness might well have gone to the heart of the issue and explained how the defendant was culturally motivated to conceal her pathology, but that he took such efforts in account. The barrister had been attempting to lead him down that path of admitting that the competencies were more an artifact of cultural values than substantive abilities. Then the issue of translators came up. Although the expert never gave a one-sentence or simple answer to a question, I have shortened his responses to go to the issues of cultural values and then of accuracy.

Q. Don't translators have cultural values too?
A. Yes.
Q. Did you do any assessment of the values the translator brought with her to the assessment?
A. No, I did not.
Q. Do you have a scientific or psychiatric reason to conclude with certainty that the values of the translator did not leak into her work and responses?
A. I don't think that happened.

At this point, the witness would have been better advised to answer the question simply that he had no scientific reason. It is impossible to know how much the values of the translator might have made their way into the answers.

An informed attorney at this point should have pursued the accuracy issue and further asked:

Q. What is the accuracy rate of translations of Cantonese interpreters?
Q. What are the sources of error in translations of Cantonese?
Q. At their very best and very worst, how well do translators capture the essence of another language?

Data exist to suggest that translators may not be very reliable. In work supported by the National Center for State Courts in the United States, Hewitt (1999) reported startlingly low hit rates of 70% at their best and well below 50% at their worst. Such losses in accuracy are never explicitly clear or available to the examiner who uses an individual translator.

For all evaluations dependent on translations, four implications are present:

1. Do not operate on the assumption that translations are literally and completely accurate. Instead, look for large

and consistent themes and do not overvalue individual replies to questions or implications that follow.

2. Become aware yourself of the cultural context in which the evaluee is located. Do this by firsthand study and consultation.

3. Spend time talking with the translator about his or her background, bicultural knowledge, and skills.

4. Depend heavily on collateral sources of information, such as records and other persons' input.

Even though the essential issue has been translations, a broader implication about cultural knowledge may be drawn as well. When clients from India for example, are interviewed in the United States, it is possible to miss powerful and nonobvious cultural factors that affect forensic and clinical judgments. Let me present such information from my own experience.

When I lived in Bangalore and Madras, I had been puzzled by a common event. Various scholars asked to meet with me to seek out my opinions. When we met, they spoke for hours about who they were and what good work they did. My opinions were never sought nor was there an opportunity for me to participate. In another context, I often asked for directions in India, and inquired if a particular direction was where I should go. Only after many wrong journeys did I discover that the cultural mandate among South Indians to be helpful led people to say yes and smile, even if they did not understand me or know the location of my destination. The related principles of making positive impressions and conformity to inquiries apply to assessing Indian clients.

It has been even more difficult for me to uncover the implicit cultural, normative, and language values associated with persons from Great Britain, New Zealand, and Australia. Without documenting these discrepancies, let me simply note that implicit differences in expectations and social desirability affect accuracy of our communication more than most assessors can identify.

THE MAXIM: *The credibility of expert opinion hinges on the accuracy of the evaluations on which that opinion is based. Inaccurate translations may cloud the accuracy of those evaluations. Take the responsibility to go beyond taking translations at face value.*

❧ 32 ❧

Empathy Dilemmas

WAITING UNTIL THE CLOSING MINUTES of the expert witness tutorial I had been leading, a reflective psychologist spoke to me of an empathy dilemma. The other participants had spoken of their anxieties about testifying and problems with cross-examinations. The group and I had offered guidance to the woman who felt inept when testifying, to the man whose general goodwill and warmth became replaced with an off-putting edginess on the stand, and to the participants who felt like professional imposters when they spoke up.

What happened to him, this quiet psychologist explained, is that he cared too deeply about the men and women he was evaluating for their various personal injury claims. Many of these people had been hurt in workplace or automobile accidents. A few had been harassed at work or attacked. In the course of his evaluations, he was moved by their losses and touched by their difficulties in trying to return to normal lives. For many of them, he found no signs of the neurological

154

impairments their attorneys had asserted in legal claims. When he wrote reports with such negative findings, and especially when he testified about them, he had a personal problem with his professional actions. He wanted these persons he had evaluated to improve their lives. His testimony of no neuropsychological impairments left him ill at ease. He felt guilty and unhappy, as he testified about findings and opinions that would potentially influence the court or jury to rule against the plaintiffs.

"I don't like being in this situation," he explained. "I don't like seeing these people whom I have evaluated hearing my testimony. And I think my dislike and unhappiness can be seen and makes my testimony less effective."

A second person with an empathy dilemma was a law enforcement officer who also had waited to talk to me after a workshop. He had participated little, but now said that he had a court date in 3 weeks about which he was really scared. Once the workshop ended, we talked for a long time about his dilemma.

In the large urban agency in which he worked, this officer had risen to being the interrogator of choice. More than any other officer, he had a history of successful interrogation of suspects and he brought out remarkably complete and condemning confessions. Unlike many other interrogators, he never implied threats or made promises of likely leniency for confessions. His style was to bond with the suspects and to find authentic connections, personal connections that led to a comfortable mutuality that then led to trust and, from the guilty, that led to confessions. I was impressed with his emotional depth and skill.

In a forthcoming case he was going to be testifying about a 17-hour interrogation over 2 days he had conducted with a young man who had kidnapped, assaulted, and brutally killed the young daughter from a politically well-known family. Hundreds of reporters would be present at the trial. The

155

confession was the main piece of evidence for the prosecution, and the videotape of this interrogation would be played with this investigator on the stand. During the interrogation, the defendant had come to trust this officer. The confession had come about because the investigator had convinced the defendant that it was the right thing to do, and the investigator had used several unconventional methods. During the interrogation, the suspect wrote a detailed letter to the parents of the victim, apologizing and asking forgiveness for what he had done. The investigator had promised to tell the suspect's parents what the suspect had done, to help them understand and to lessen the devastation they would feel. He did this in person later, returning to meet with them several times.

Four things concerned him about his testimony. First, he was afraid that he would come across as inappropriate as an officer because of the visible and personal way in which he had truly bonded with this suspect. Second, he was concerned he would be seen by the press and public as manipulatively having made statements to soften the suspect into confessing. Third, he was concerned that his own continuing feelings of attachment to this man would come out. Finally, he was concerned about what he would do while sitting on the stand for the 17 hours during which the prosecution would be playing the video of the interrogation.

For both of these men caught in dilemmas about their roles and empathy, I suggested, first, that it would be useful to reexamine what they do. Many professionals find that they have slipped into activities that do not fit closely with their values and personal needs. Some element of that discrepancy was true with them.

The second and major suggestion was about testifying; they should stay closely to descriptions and behaviors. If they allowed their own feelings, attitudes, or thoughts to surface, then they could be in an untenable situation. It is never necessary that witnesses lay out all they are thinking and feeling.

Now, if these two men were comfortable with their empathic reactions to the plaintiff and to the defendant, respectively, then my advice would have been different. Saying that he empathized with the pain and hurt of the individual about whom he was testifying would have been fine for the psychologist, as he testified there were no observable deficits. Describing the emotions of the defendant would normally have been acceptable for the investigator. But these options were not acceptable in their cases. The reason to stay with descriptions of statements and behaviors is to limit the presentation of one's own problematic feelings.

Should witnesses in general allow empathic experiences to be visible? It depends on the nature of the empathy. If it is conflicted and mixed, then witnesses may wish to be cautious, restrained, and opaque. Conversely, many trials concern issues in which parties have been harmed or distressed. A controlled but genuine empathy by expert witnesses can humanize them and make their testimony more acceptable and credible.

THE MAXIM: *Keep testimony coolly descriptive about your behaviors and about the litigants, when you may be excessively empathic or emotional about the case. Otherwise, allow modest degrees of empathic expression and limited personal feelings to appear in your testimony in order to be real and human about the issues.*

❧ 33 ❧

Headline Testimony

MOST WITNESSES GO ABOUT PROVIDING their observations and findings in quiet and unremarkable ways. For example, involuntary commitments and routine tort actions are little noted except by the parties. Most criminal cases generate minimal publicity because there are too many trials, too little interest, and few if any reporters. Some sensationalist or social policy aspect occasionally leads the media to pay attention, and the public to care about specific trials. Still, few trials make national headlines. About two times a month, such headline-grabbing cases are featured in TV, Internet, and newspaper reports, cases in which the public is led to think that something important is at stake. These are not necessarily criminal cases: think of the Microsoft monopoly trial, product liability actions, and suits against tobacco and asbestos companies. However, the greatest coverage is usually allocated to dramatic murder trials. When expert and lay witness alike emerge as foreground figures and in the national spotlight in these cases, along comes fame or notoriety. The pressure from the media for information can be intense. Appelbaum (1984) put it this way:

> The public's appetite for information about crime, its perpetrators, and its victims appears almost insatiable. The more gruesome the crime and the more intimate the details revealed, the greater the level of public interest. Since forensic clinicians are likely to be involved in the most shocking cases, and to be possessed of the most titillating pieces of information, they are often assiduously courted by the media and implored to share their knowledge. In addition to the ever-present newspaper and magazine stories, recent months have witnessed television specials devoted to crimes involving mental illness, in which forensic evaluators spoke in great detail about persons they had examined. (p. 296)

Public attention associated with headline trials can stay with key witnesses their whole lives long. More than 20 years after the attempted murder trial of John Hinckley, Jr. for attempting to assassinate then-President Ronald Reagan, witness for the prosecution Park Dietz is sometimes remembered for his testimony. In a similar vein, expert witnesses are still remembered from the O. J. Simpson and the Jeffrey Dahmer trials, and not just about what they testified on the stand. The media can elicit public statements that have not been thought out well in terms of content and issues of confidentiality and privilege. Grisso (1990) portrayed the media demands in these terms:

> A clinical psychologist has just testified about her evaluation of a defendant in a notorious criminal trial. At the end of the day, she steps out of the quiet courtroom onto the courthouse steps, where she is confronted by blinding lights and a wall of waving microphones and minicams. She is asked to comment on the expert testimony she has given. (p. 427)

159

Both Grisso (1990) and Appelbaum (1984) have argued convincingly that the defendants have expectations that the expert will reveal content only in the legal context. Confidentiality may still be seen to apply in terms of the media. The essence of the issue is that " . . . the examiner has an independent ethical obligation that goes beyond the examinee's consent. The examiner should refuse to participate in media interviews requested by the examinee if the totality of risks associated with the disclosure convinces the examiner that it should be avoided" (Grisso, 1990, p. 431). The risks identified by Grisso include common media distortions, the impromptu nature of media interviews, and the compromising of both the legal process and the perceived objectivity of the expert. Furthermore, there is the hazard of the residual labeling of the witness.

Testifying in headline cases can follow a witness in a negative way. Consider these examples. An expert mental health witness came to be known for his unlikely conclusion that a rare fugue state led the defendant to kill a notorious public figure. Controversial testimony has been offered that persons in a psychotic state with command hallucinations may have (and also may not have) appreciated fully the wrongfulness of a murder act. Methods of assessment marginal to mainstream knowledge have been used in forming mental health and other expert opinions. The ripple effects from famous cases and media experts spread out for a long time.

I do not want to be famous as the psychologist who testified about a movie star who is an alleged murderer. It is a bad variation on being a one-trick pony, in which a pop singer is known only for one song, an actor for one film, an author for one novel and little else for the rest of their lives. Most headline cases that come the way of health professionals are of short duration in professional lives and have modest impact, such as the following case.

The 1963 bombing of the 16th Street Baptist Church in Birmingham, Alabama killed four young Black girls. In that era of marches and protests, violence and murders, this event was one of the most heinous acts. Trials of the three primary defendants ended in the 1960s in hung juries until at the close of the 20th century, charges were again filed and criminal cases began again to go to trial. William Blanton had been convicted and sentenced for the bombing when Bobby Frank Cherry, allegedly a Ku Klux Klan member, was indicted.[12] He was evaluated in 2001 for competency to stand trial, and on the basis of expert testimony that he suffered from vascular dementia, was found not competent. After a stay in the state forensic hospital, Cherry was returned to court in 2002 for a hearing about whether he had been restored to competency. With newspaper reporters clamoring and television cameras whirring, two psychologists testified that he had been malingering before, and was indeed competent to stand trial.

Both expert witnesses[13] described the level of scrutiny as higher than anything they had experienced before. It was "like big brother looking over my shoulder." Remember, the issue was whether vascular dementia interfered with functional competency to stand trial, and not guilt or innocence.

One expert testified that Cherry scored as a malingerer on the Test of Memory Malingering (TOMM). Only 3 of 43 persons with "dementia" in the norms had scored in Cherry's range. The defense attorney then asked a series of questions about these 3 persons out of the 43.

---

[12] The best among several books about this case is *Carry Me Home* (McWhorter, 2002).

[13] The witnesses were Al Whitehead and Kathleen Ronan. They generously gave permission to use their comments and testimony.

Q1. Doctor, what is the bell curve in psychology? (answered).

Q2. Doctor, assume for the purposes of the court that a normal distribution was in effect for these three persons. Now isn't it true you have no way of knowing for certain whether Mr. Cherry would be more like one of the three than like the others?

A1. The three persons with dementia were outliers.

Q3. Yes, but can't bell curves apply to outliers too?

Q4. Can't both normal and abnormal people be part of normal curves?

In this effort to obscure testimony, the attorney asked reasonable-appearing questions of the genre illustrated above, and the expert made a serious attempt to answer. In retrospect, his judgment was that he was too caught up in detail. A broader overview with less detail was in order for the expert, perhaps explaining repeatedly that norms are not the same as normal distributions.

Testimony in many famous cases has now become archived and available through Court TV. I have viewed many times the testimony of the mental health experts in the Jeffrey Dahmer trial. One witness's testimony continues to make me shudder as I watch his inappropriate assertions mixed with condescending attitudes, a disastrous combination.

Not everybody has an option to accept or decline headline cases. Professionals who work for agencies and institutions may be assigned to cases. For other professionals thinking about taking on such work, I suggest caution. Try not to pursue it for the egotistical reasons of being known. Instead, make such decisions on the basis of genuine expertise and prior experience. Anticipate that your work may be open to both public and professional discourse. Do not be seduced by the pull from the media. "Being seen frequently on the six o'clock news in advocacy roles may involve considerable long-range risks to the expert's reputation, in that judges (and the public from whom jurors are drawn) may come to perceive the examiner as biased and less credible" (Grisso, 1990, p. 433). Be comfortable with stating that you have no comment and will not be available to discuss the case or your assessment.

THE MAXIM: *Headline testimony is risky business.*
If options are available, turn down all such invitations
to be involved unless you are clearly suited for the task.
Approach publicity and the media with caution and
discretion, even if the evaluee has given permission.
Master saying "no comment."

❦ 34 ❧

Distrusting Experts

MOST CITIZENS AND JURORS have a reasoned approach to judging the objectivity of expert witnesses. They listen with care to testimony, they absorb as much as they can of what often is technical information, they size up how believable the expert is—based in part on subjective factors—and draw a conclusion. Some forensic experts are considerably more skeptical than the public of the objectivity of expert witnesses. One good example is in the commentary of Dr. Michael Lamport Commons, who wrote the following

> Most people, when they are paid to take the perspective of a client, will become biased in favor of their clients. This is not unlike the bias that develops in any psychophysical detection study. Payoff or frequency of presentation of a particular stimulus always biases the subject. Subjects are not corrupt people per se. But outcome affects choice under uncertainty.

People defend such biased decision making. This is a well-known phenomenon called cognitive dissonance. After a while, people who role-play a lawyer acquire response biases. When I give them moral dilemmas, they do not appear particularly corrupt because they do not have to choose a side.

Many expert witnesses argue that to work both for the defense and the prosecution in different cases decreases the amount of bias. I argue that it makes expert witnesses more like lawyers. It speeds up the rate of acquiring a bias for a particular case. Even if one bills for just hours and not whether or not one supports the lawyers' view, bias develops because of the contingencies of the world.

There are two competing contingencies: that of winning and that of desirability as a witness. One wins more cases if one is less biased. In the other contingency, some bias helps business. Lawyers often like to work with people who agree with them.

One thing that bothers me about the notion that expert witnesses are whores is that whores are very professional. They do not get sexually excited by their clients. I am not sure that is true of expert witnesses.[14]

The views held by Dr. Commons are, if you will put up with my choice of words, commonly held. A pull toward bias surely does exist. The task of the expert is, first, to be aware of the obvious and nonobvious ways in which such pulls are present. It sometimes takes the form of desire to please. Sometimes, it appears because the cause seems just. Sometimes, it takes the form of moving overly early to an

---

[14]Michael Lamport Commons, personal communication, May 5, 1998.

opinion, and discarding additional and nonconfirmatory information.

The second task is to keep neutrality as an explicit, immediate, and highest priority. With mild huffiness, during pretrial meetings I have asked retaining attorneys if they are trying to convince me about what I should say in court; I ask this question as an explicit means of clarifying my commitment to neutrality.

Third, Dr. Commons asserts that one of the toxic things that happens to experts is that they become like attorneys. In one sense, that is desirable. They surely should know thoroughly the legal context of their assessment or testimony. In the broader sense, it is unacceptable to advocate alongside the attorney.

Fourth, Dr. Commons takes the position that being retained at different times both by the prosecution (or plaintiffs) and defense accelerates bias. I disagree. The integrity of the expert stands apart from who retains the expert. It is possible to be objective whether retained only by one side or the other or both. Objectivity lies in approach, methodology, and scholarly or professional accountability. I do not join any automatic condemnation of experts on the basis of who retains them.

Next, the word *winning* is used to describe the involvement of experts. Use of "winning" does conjure up an advocacy posture. Experts never win nor lose. Attorneys, clients, and the state may win or lose. If experts think of themselves as winning or losing a case, then they are indeed committed to the adversarial process. One participates. One testifies. One gives an opinion within the reach of one's competence. Period.

It is possible to construe testimony as succeeding, in the sense that one succeeds in presenting case information and findings in a clear and understandable way. That goal is altogether proper.

Finally, Dr. Commons suggests that expert witnesses are less professional and more personally involved and sexually excited than "whores" (presumably he is referring to prostitutes) are in their work. I know this is intended as a piece of wit as much as substance, but it still merits a comment. It serves us ill to so condemn all expert witnesses. A few may indeed be easily moved to an adversarial posture. However, we should consider each expert on the basis of his or her own performance. In my observations, few fall in this "bought" subjective group. Even when they disagree with my findings, most are committed and conscientious professionals.

THE MAXIM: *Experts should not be surprised by negative perceptions by other professionals that they are biased. Such possible accusations are all the more reason to perform at high levels of knowledge and accountability.*

❧ 35 ❧

Lawyer Intrusions

I HAVE LONG ADMIRED A PARTICULAR LAWYER who has dedicated his career to helping the disadvantaged, and fighting against racism. I have known him in passing for some time, but just before I started working with him on a case, I had listened to him reading his autobiography on a book on tape and had seen him on television speaking for a cause—unrelated to the case—in which I deeply believe. Throughout the continuous static of death threats against him, he has spoken out clearly for justice in a dedicated and effective way. Perhaps that is why his request so influenced me.

This attorney had been a passive participant in the murder defense until a few weeks before the trial, and now joined in actively. The case was a difficult one: unequivocal evidence of a shooting leading to the victim's death, and, at that point, the defense was aiming at life without parole as the best possible outcome. The more likely outcome was the death penalty. I had been asked to evaluate the defendant about his drug intoxication and life history, to be used as part of mitigation testimony prior to sentencing. We were talking about the test results.

"Have you looked at the MMPI [Minnesota Multiphasic Personality Inventory] results yet?" he asked me, in his new role as co-counsel for the defendant.

"No," I replied. The 50 pages of profiles, supplemental scales, and report had just arrived. "But I plan to look at them later today."

"Don't!" he instructed. "I don't want them admitted in evidence."

When I explained that I needed to use the MMPI, the attorney said two things. First, he wanted to have the case before the jury right before Christmas so that the jury would be in a charitable mood. If I used my report, the state would be entitled to see it and get their own expert, and the trial would be postponed until after Christmas.

Second, the attorney explained that he had full confidence in my ability to draw on my extended interview and examination of collateral information. I put the MMPI profile, data, and report in an envelope and set it aside. Over the next week I spoke at different times with the lawyer and his co-counsel about my planned use of the materials. Each time, they patiently explained that it would undermine their case strategy. I finally acquiesced.

Christmas fell on a Friday. The case was scheduled to begin the week before and it was anticipated that the case would wrap up on December 24. The jury selection began slowly, and the pretrial publicity was so extensive that a jury could not be struck. The trial was rescheduled for January.

Once again, I stated that I needed the MMPI. Once again, they replied that it did not fit into the way they wished to pursue the case. This time, I insisted: "If you require that

I not look at the MMPI," I said in what I like to think was a determined tone of voice, "I am afraid I will have to withdraw from being involved in this case. I will not bill you for my time. I cannot continue in good conscience when I cannot maintain the standard of practice for such evaluations." I meant it, of course. I felt empty-handed without test results to accompany my other information.

After a hasty discussion, they agreed. I looked. The MMPI-2 profile was not valid. The T-score for F was 115. Although some scale results were interesting, they added little to what I already knew. Then, on the day I was scheduled to testify, I waited for 5 hours to be called to the stand. They had been pleased with how the case had gone without my testimony and were not certain whether to call me. Finally, the case wrapped up and went to the jury without the defense calling me to testify.

Three elements of this case are of interest. First, the lawyer intruded into what was a professional decision about methods of evaluation. I erred by capitulating at first, even though later I gained enough clarity to stay with my original plan of evaluation.

Second, such issues should be worked out a priori. I had described the evaluation plan to the first lawyer. When the famous lawyer came on board, the oral agreement had faded into background. Although not an absolute prerequisite, it is a good idea to indicate in writing the methods to be used.

Finally, our professional crises often turn into practical insignificance. As in some other instances, this MMPI and planned testimony had no utility. Although I did hold that the MMPI-2 was the preferred psychometric method of personality and psychopathology assessment, my insistence made no actual difference in any aspect of the case. I reflect on the experience as a humility lesson.

THE MAXIM: *Evaluators and not attorneys need to define their customary standards of professional practice. Stay committed to what you do and how you do it, even in the face of attorney pressures.*

Clear Boundaries of Testimony

FACED WITH WHAT APPEARED TO BE a certain conviction of their client on capital murder charges, the team of attorneys approached me with a request. Their client would soon be awaiting a recommendation by the jury for the death penalty or life with parole. They asked me to testify about these two issues.

First, they wanted me to testify about how bad the conditions would be on death row. Their reasoning was that this information about harsh and punitive death row conditions would lead the jury to feel sorry for the family of the defendant (but not the defendant himself) if the defendant was given the death penalty. The attorneys knew I had worked as a prison psychologist in an institution with a death row, and that I had inspected or visited death rows in several states, occasionally writing or speaking about my findings (Brodsky, 1982, 2002; Brodsky, Zapf, & Boccaccini, 2001). Therefore, they asked me to testify about what I had observed about life on death row.

Second, they had read a just released lengthy report about how three-fourths of all death penalty sentences are eventually overturned on appeal or through other legal means. They asked if I would talk about this study, which was not known to me until they handed me a copy. Their rationale was to have me admitted as an expert who had read the study so that the results of the study itself could be admitted in evidence. The high rate of overturning death sentences would, in their thinking, deter the jury from recommending capital punishment.

When attorneys approach experts for assistance or to testify, they always have an agenda. Often, the agenda is implicit and not clearly stated. In the present instance the attorneys were reasonably explicit in their goals for my expert testimony. In all instances in which one is approached to testify, it is useful to think through the request. Some witnesses simply accept the working assumptions of the attorneys without questioning them. Once the assumptions are accepted, experts may find themselves in a position in which they are absolutely committed to attorney goals for their testimony. As time goes by, without thinking about it, witnesses may find that the attorneys' position becomes their own. In a related context, Stephen King (1998), in his novel *Bag of Bones*, wrote about the perceived alliance between client and attorney:

> There's something oddly comforting about talk-
> ing to a legal guy once the billable-hours clock
> has started running; you have passed the magical
> point at which a lawyer becomes your lawyer.
> Your lawyer is warm, your lawyer is sympathetic,
> your lawyer makes notes on a yellow pad and
> nods in all the right places. Most of the questions
> your lawyer asks are questions you can answer.
> And if you can't, your lawyer will help you find

173

> a way to do so, by God. Your lawyer is always on your side. Your enemies are his enemies. To him, you are never shit but always Shinola. (pp. 167–168)

The avid, admiring, chock-a-block attention the attorneys paid to me in this case is consistent with what sometimes has happened in other cases. I might have indeed felt like Shinola, if only I knew what Shinola was.[15] However, with all the goodwill and courtesy I could muster, I resisted their requests and set a boundary past which I would not testify.

The capital punishment study, I explained, was legal research and not psychological research. It was not research I conducted nor was it research I relied on. If they needed someone to testify about that study, I explained, they should get a legal scholar. I declined the invitation. Furthermore, I raised the issue that if there are effective appeal mechanisms for correcting death penalty decisions, this might make the jury more rather than less prone to sentence the defendant to death.

The other issue I had been asked to address was the harshness of death row confinement. Although the boundary of my competence was not a concern for me here, the rationale was a concern. I suggested that my research and experience related to the harshness of prison life outside death row in this state correctional system might be more useful. After all, if the jurors concluded that life imprisonment in a punitive correctional system was a severe penalty, they might not feel as much need for the death penalty in their deliberations.

The attorneys listened with care, accepted what I said, and changed their requests about the nature of my testimony

---

[15] Since I first wrote this, it has come to my attention that Shinola is a no-longer manufactured brand of shoe polish.

in these suggested ways. They said they felt better about what they would ask me. I know I did.

◈

THE MAXIM: *Establish the boundaries of testimony and expertise, and structure accordingly how and about what you will testify.*

◈

175

❦ 37 ❦

(Not) Offering Advice

A S MURDER TRIALS GO, this one was low key. The victim had a record of previous arrests and had been recently released from many years in prison. The community was distant and disinterested in him as well as disinterested in the often arrested adult murder victim. The judge was anxious to clear the docket of the whole matter. After many delays, the trial was scheduled to begin the next week. I received a phone call from the defense attorney who had retained me months earlier to evaluate the defendant. "The state has requested a continuance because they are not prepared," the attorney said to me. "The judge asked me and my co-counsel whether we agree to it. We haven't decided yet. Do you think it is a good idea?" "I don't know," I replied. "You see," he went on, "the

---

Patricia Griffin offered helpful comments on an early draft of this chapter.

176

prosecution is not prepared. Really not prepared. That might give us an advantage at trial. But if we wait, we might be able to cut a better deal. You have a good sense of what the defendant is like. What would you do? Would you agree to the continuance?"

Part of my response was that I did not know enough about the legal issues and the overall case. I stated that I was knowledgeable only about the part with which I was involved, the psychological evaluation. My declining of the invitation may have been the responsible thing to do. After all, the issues were embedded in a variety of legal and strategic factors well beyond the range of my expertise.

However, I did have a professional opinion about what was happening with the attorney and I did have a personal opinion about what was convenient for me. My professional opinion was that this reasonably well-prepared defense attorney should proceed with the trial the next week because continued time in jail would not serve the defendant well. In this mostly rural county in which the largest town had a population of 20,000, the states' attorneys and defense attorney were unusually friendly and part of the same social circle, even by rural standards of fraterniza-tion. My thought was that the defense wanted to defer to the request out of friendly consideration for valued persons in the professional community. I was aware that one of the attorneys in the District Attorney's office was the sister of the lead defense attorney.

I had a personal opinion as well, which I did express in a mild manner. I had already set aside the substantial block of time during the next week to testify. It would be inconvenient to reschedule things. However, I had not been asked what was best for me. By deliberately not offering legal advice to the lawyer, I had the intention of staying within the boundaries of my work. Still, I did tell him that the current scheduling of the trial was desirable in terms of my time commitments.

When I was brought into this capital murder case, it was as a mitigation expert witness. Anticipating a guilty verdict, the attorney had begun to prepare for the sentencing phase. He asked me to evaluate the impact on the defendant of having been confined for many years in the worst of the Alabama state prisons. I found no appreciable impact. I did reach other conclusions. The defendant had no signs of prior violence and minimal indications of aggressive attitudes, angry feelings, or present or future violent behaviors. Once I suggested to the attorney that he might want to call me to the stand and ask me about these results, he looked to me for other advice. In other words, I had already acted in a manner to influence trial strategy. My limited advice in response to the current question in terms of what was best for my own schedule was noted with courtesy. Then the attorney disregarded my reply and agreed to the continuence.

Yet there are many instances in which retained experts can and should offer advice within the scope of their work to attorneys. Here are four instances in which trial advice to attorneys is responsible and useful.

1. How to conceptualize and approach the underlying issues related to your work.

2. What questions not to ask and what questions to ask.

3. The logical ways in which your testimony should unfold.

4. The questions likely to be asked on cross that are better asked on direct.

Many experts attribute depth of knowledge and understanding to the attorneys who retain them. A few masterful attorneys have such a lucid and cohesive grasp of the law and of trial practice that such attributions are justified. But there are not many such attorneys.

A few attorneys are at the opposite extreme, with murky understandings of the law and a haphazard, impromptu approach to trial practice. The majority of attorneys are somewhere in the middle, with areas of selective strength and gaps as well. When the ethical issues of offering advice are resolved (see Brodsky, 1999), these mid-knowledge attorneys can benefit from expert advice. Take this actual scenario from pretrial discussions and consultation in a case.

Me:	What is your theory of the case?
Attorney (A):	The defendant went along with the other defendant. He had not meant to kill the victim but only tie him up.
Me:	What beliefs do you want the jurors to acquire?
A:	Well, I want the judge to rule that the statements during the interrogations are not admissible. And I want them to find for the defendant.
Me:	Yes, but what specific ideas about the case do you want the jurors to acquire?
A:	Well, it would be good if they understood that because the defendant keeps changing his story does not mean that he is guilty.
Me:	In that case, let us work on the theory of the case related to that issue. From what I can tell the motivations for changing the story are fears of being punished, an effort to improve his story when he retells it, and some genuine confusion about what happened. Let's start with his fear of being punished as a way to develop this part of the theory of the case.

When the experts are offering testimony, they have an obligation to themselves to promote the communication and understanding. Sometimes that means educating the attorneys, structuring the direct examination, and developing one's own theory of the mental health aspects of the case.

When should the expert offer advice and when should one refrain from offering advice? Gentle suggestions may always be offered toward the objective of promotion of the best in your testimony. Attorneys should know how you think about your testimony and what essential questions should be asked. When attorneys leap into unanticipated content during direct examinations, it is as much the fault of the expert witness as of the attorney. Take care of yourself and your testimony by being proactive: suggest, encourage, and even direct the attorney.

Finally, as a testifying expert, do not offer advice beyond the limits of your competence and role, no matter how much it appears to promote your beliefs about justice. Excessive professional stretches may especially occur in response to requests for legal, procedural, or evidentiary advice.[16]

THE MAXIM: *Freely offer advice about substantive content of your testimony to attorneys who have retained you. As a witness, be cautious about being drawn into inappropriate advice giving.*

---

[16] Experts who also have law degrees have an even finer line to walk because their roles can easily become complex and differentiated responsibilities to the court and to the retaining attorneys can become ambiguous.

❧ 38 ❧

Token Experts

ONE PSYCHOLOGIST OFTEN CHATS WITH ME by e-mail about her forensic practice. She wrote to me regarding her concerns about being retained.

> I am becoming more aware of a business problem related to civil practice. Being in a relatively small metropolitan area in a small state, I am one of the few forensic experts at my level. My present policy is to get a deposit at the time of retention, and then work against that deposit for the initial fees. The problem I have had is that lately several firms have retained me with the sole intention of depriving the other side of my services. They give me the deposit, don't give me any work to do, then ask for their deposit back, and I end up with bupkis.[17]

---

[17] *Bupkis* is a Yiddish word that literally means beans, but in practical use means a quantity or payment so small that it is insignificant or insulting.

> I am considering having the deposit changed
> to a nonrefundable retainer, so that if they decide
> not to use my services, it would be forfeited any-
> way. From my perspective, it would be a way of
> getting paid for sitting on the sidelines of what
> could have been a large case.

"What do you think about this?" she asked. "Is it ethical?" This psychologist raised an interesting issue. The idea of the nonrefundable retainer may not be unethical, but it has an unsavory quality. I had an alternate proposal.

When you are asked to be involved in a case, request a copy of the complaint, documents, or other materials about the case. Tell the firm you will review these materials so you know if you wish to be retained. After all, it is an ethical mandate to practice only within one's area of competence, and only to accept referrals if they are assignments you might indeed eventually agree to undertake.

Indicate to the attorney your minimum fee for reviewing files, charges, and complaints—perhaps payment for 4 hours of your time—and request that the fee and files be sent simultaneously. The appeal of this alternative is that it involves doing work for the fee.

A message came back. This psychologist argued that the real issue is what the retaining parties get for their money, when there is a nonrefundable retainer and no work performed. She held that the retaining firms deprive her of the opportunity to work for the other side, a situation that might result in a significant fee. It is the lost opportunity to earn fees which is of value; that is what the retaining firm is purchasing. In other words, the nonrefundable retainer compels the firms to decide if getting her out of the game is really worth it. If so, they pay the fee. If not, the expert is still in the game.

I have an objection to such thinking. The expert does not know if she would even be asked to provide expert knowledge by the opposing side. Furthermore, even if retained, she does not know for certain that she will not be asked by the retaining firm to work on the case.

Instead of charging a nonrefundable retainer, why not go to the heart of the matter and charge a retention fee to allow the attorney to list her as a retained expert. Then if the attorney does use her, the cost of the initial work may be deducted from that explicit fee.

When I run into this problem, I do ask for retainers, but never nonrefundable ones. Sometimes I am not retained. I may lose some income, but the goodwill generated by this principled choice is worth it.

THE MAXIM: *In small communities, ethical boundaries are often troublesome. Experts should have their policies about retention responsibly defined well in advance of being retained.*

❧ 39 ❧

Expert Panels

W HEN I WAS ASKED TO BE ON AN EXPERT PANEL, I was not sure what to expect. All of my forensic evaluations to that point had been performed individually, almost all as a result of being retained by one side or the other, and every now and then, directly by the court. Our panel was appointed by a federal district judge to address the competency to stand trial of a defendant who had been awaiting trial for years.

Two competency examinations had preceded ours. One evaluation concluded without reservation that the apparently retarded defendant had been unable to understand the most basic elements in his trial and was not competent. The second, and equally qualified, evaluator concluded that the defendant was competent and malingering, in part because the man transparently tried to present himself as intellectually dim and emotionally disturbed.

Three of us were asked to serve on the panel. The other two psychologists had little forensic experience. One specialized in family work and the other in psychotherapy. Both, however, were prominent in the city in which the court was located. I was probably chosen for a personal reason. Some years earlier, when the judge was a U.S. Attorney, we had occasion to work together.

Before the evaluation, I met for an hour with the judge in his large corner office in the massive federal courthouse. We talked about some of his recent controversial decisions, about people we knew in common, and about some personal matters, too. We also talked about the case. What the judge did not quite say, but what I inferred, was that three of us doing one evaluation and offering one joint opinion (which was part of the order appointing us) would resolve the court's conundrum of handling the two contradictory prior assessments.

The three of us on the panel had never worked together before. We were instructed to meet as a team with the defendant for the entire time of the evaluation. We three psychologists sat with the defendant around a table in the jail, asking questions in turn. Situational and examiner effects can affect the responses of any person being evaluated. Surely, the fact that the defendant was outnumbered and surrounded by the three of us, each going out of our way to be respectful of the others' approaches, made the assessment different than a conventional single examiner situation.

Because the court required that we come up with a single written report, we had no structure to form independent opinions, and then reconcile them. In fact, the court seemed to want no such independence. The requirement was an integrated evaluation, methodology, conclusion, opinion, and report.

At times it was awkward. One of the other experts used a test I would not use in a competency evaluation (the Bender-Gestalt). Some of the questions seemed to be off-task for competency issues. We did use the Everington CAST*MR

(Competence Assessment to Stand Trial for Defendants With Mental Retardation; Everington & Luckasson, 1992) for assessing competency with low-functioning persons. Afterward, our discussion was congenial, but I wondered if the other experts deferred a bit to me because of my forensic experience and because I had practiced longer.

We submitted our report. The judge accepted our conclusion that the defendant did not meet the psychological threshold for competency, cancelled the request for us to testify, and declared the defendant not competent.

There were several elements in serving on the panel that I liked. Even though a small, not very still voice in the back of my mind told me we should think independently, it was nice—very nice—to discuss the person's responses with peers, to compare data and responses, and to come to a consensus. It was reassuring to see how much we agreed. The idea of writing a joint report was initially alien to me. I drafted it, and received thoughtful, intelligent feedback. The final report was better than what I would have done on my own. Finally, the use of the panel and the appointment by the court provided a context isolated from adversarial process and more focused on the job. It is not that I, or the other panel members, seek to please retaining attorneys. But it was pleasant to have not even a hint of pressure or expectations.

THE MAXIM: *One cannot seek out appointments on expert panels, but when it happens, it can be a learning opportunity in consensus and autonomy, insulated from customary adversarial events.*

ATTORNEY EXTRAPOLATIONS
AND DEMANDS

❦ 40 ❦

Yes or No Demands

THE SPRING OF 1960 BROUGHT TO GARDEN CITY, Kansas the murder trial of Richard Hickock and Perry Edward Smith for killing Herbert and Bonnie Clutter and their children Nancy and Kenyon in their home in Holcomb, Kansas the previous November. Among the details of the trial, as reported by Truman Capote (1965) in his best-selling book *In Cold Blood,* were the questions put to psychiatrist W. Mitchell Jones, the head of the forensic unit at Larned State Hospital. The following excerpts illustrate how this expert witness was severely limited in what he was permitted to say.[18]

---

[18] Capote was immaculately careful in his reporting of the factual information of the murders, the subsequent events in the lives of Hickock and Smith, and the trial. I am indebted to Jessica Lacher-Feldman of the Hoole Special Collections Library at The University of Alabama for her research into the facts of the case and into the documentation of the trial by Capote.

188

(Attorney Harrison Smith) "Approximately how many murderers have you dealt with?"

(Dr. W. Mitchell Jones) "About twenty-five."

"Doctor, I would like to ask you if you know my client, Richard Eugene Hickock?"

"I do."

"Have you had occasion to examine him professionally?"

"Yes, sir . . . I made a psychiatric examination of Mr. Hickock."

"Based upon your examination, do you have an opinion as to whether Richard Eugene Hickock knew right from wrong at the time of the commission of the crime?"

The witness, a stout man of twenty-eight with a moon-shaped but intelligent, subtly delicate face, took a deep breath, as though to equip himself for a prolonged reply—which the judge then cautioned him he must not make: "You may answer the question yes or no, Doctor. Limit your answer to yes or no."

"Yes."

"And what is your opinion?"

"I think that within the usual definitions Mr. Hickock did know right from wrong." Confined as he was by the McNaghten Rule . . . a formula quite color-blind to any gradations between black and white, Dr. Jones was impotent to answer otherwise. But of course the response was a let-down for Hickock's attorney, who helplessly asked, "Can you qualify that answer?" (Capote, 1965, pp. 293–294)

It was helpless because the prosecution successfully objected that Kansas law allowed no response beyond a yes or no reply. The doctor had been prepared to describe Hickock's history of a serious head injury, of emotional abnormality, and the possibility that his severe character disorder was the product of organic brain damage. Later in the trial, Dr. Jones

189

was recalled by Arthur Fleming, attorney for Perry Smith, who asked:

> "From your conversations and examination of Perry Edward Smith, do you have an opinion as to whether he knew right from wrong at the time of the offense involved in this action?" and once more the court admonished the witness: "Answer yes or no, do you have an opinion?"
>
> "No."
>
> Amid surprised mutters, Fleming, surprised himself, said, "You may state to the jury why you have no opinion."
>
> Green (the prosecutor) objected: "The man has no opinion, and that's *it*." Which it was, legally speaking. (Capote, 1965, p. 296)

What Dr. Jones would have said, if permitted, was that Perry Smith showed signs of severe mental illness. Smith would have been described as having a paranoid orientation to the world, poorly controlled rage, signs of a thought disorder, and emotional blandness. Dr. Jones would have concluded that a more extensive evaluation was needed but the diagnosis was "very nearly that of a paranoid schizophrenic reaction" (p. 297).

Hickock and Smith were found guilty, and were executed at Lansing State Prison in April, 1965. It is likely that nothing Dr. Jones might have said would have made a difference in the verdict and sentence. Nevertheless, his testimony reflects the common problem that affects many witnesses, both lay and expert, of dealing with demands for yes or no answers.

Typical advice for handling such absolutist demands includes saying:

- There is no yes or no answer to that question.
- It would be professionally irresponsible for me to give a yes or no answer to that question.
- Offering an admit–deny reply to complex questions, so that the part of the question that is true is acknowledged and the part that is untrue is vigorously denied.

In the case of Dr. Jones's testimony, with the constraints of this court and this judge, the steel lid on explanations would have probably remained tightly sealed. Joel Dvoskin has offered one approach that he used to answer such questions:[19]

> ... in regard to yes-no questions, I'd like to share an experience I once had, many years ago, in Federal Court. The following took place after an attorney asked a yes/no question, which I tried to answer honestly, i.e., without answering either yes or no. As best I remember. . . .
>
> Attorney: "Dr. Dvoskin, please answer the question yes or no."
>
> Dvoskin: "I will not do that."
>
> Attorney: "Your honor, will you please instruct the witness to answer the question yes or no?"
>
> Judge: "The witness will answer the question yes or no."
>
> Dvoskin: (gulp) "Your honor, I have great respect for the court, and nothing would make me happier than to do what you ask. But to do so would violate the oath that you made me take before I began my testimony, in that a yes or no answer would mislead the court, and thus would not be the whole truth."
>
> Judge: (glaring at a cowering Dvoskin) "What did you just say?"
>
> Dvoskin: "If the court wishes me to violate my oath in this manner, I will gladly do so as long as the court orders it on the record."
>
> I swear the attorney general who called me almost fainted. The judge was by then staring daggers at a sweaty, shivering expert witness who wished he was anywhere else in the whole stinking world. The clock slowed to a surrealistic

---

[19] Joel Dvoskin, personal communication, November 17, 2002.

crawl. My whole life passed before my eyes (luck-
ily I was young, so it didn't take that long.)
    Judge: "You'd better make it snappy."
    And snappy it was.

Would this technique have worked for Dr. Jones? I doubt it. Should it be a technique that other witnesses should try? Not as a first resort. Good witnesses have a substantial repertoire of possible responses; replying that a yes or no answer would violate the oath to tell the whole truth may or may not be useful, but certainly it would be lined up well behind many others in the queue of desirable answers. One hazard of such a reply is that court may think that the witness is engaging in game-playing and manipulation, and that kind of perception can undermine whatever else the witness may have to say.

❖

THE MAXIM: *Be emotionally prepared for the possibility
that some of your answers will be limited to yes or no,
but also be cognitively prepared to make the case
that a yes or no answer is simply inadequate
for the nature of the testimony.*

❖

41

Clients Next Door

I N A HEARING IN WHICH HE HAD TESTIFIED that a 15-year-old girl should not be transferred to criminal court to be tried as an adult, my colleague Robert Lyman was asked a provocative question. After his assessment, Bob had also offered the opinion that this girl was an appropriate candidate for treatment in a juvenile correctional institution, and could benefit from such treatment. These two criteria are part of the standards for transfer to adult courts established by the Supreme Court in the 1966 *Kent v. United States* decision.

The provocative question that the Assistant District Attorney asked Bob Lyman: "Would you want this girl to live next door to you as a neighbor?"

This question falls in a category I have come to think of as associative personalization. By associative, I mean that the question is associated in some loose way with the issues before the court. By personalization, I mean that the witness is asked to move from the relatively detached and objective posture of evaluating expert to that of a feeling, reacting, and involved party. The trick in such questions is that the expert is not evaluating the defendant for being a neighbor, or on other personal dimensions. When one has a chance to think about it, the question may be understood as a clever non sequitur that does not follow the testimony, although the associative link makes it appear that it does.

When asked this question, Bob Lyman replied: "If she were to become my neighbor, I would much prefer having her there after she had been treated in a juvenile facility than after she had spent time in an adult prison."

This excellent answer accepted the assumptions of the question. It was pointed and related back directly to case issues, so that the associative personalization did not work well. However, it also bought into the assumption that Bob was testifying as an expert on who should live next to him.

When Bob, another colleague, and I were engaged in a post hoc discussion of the questions and answers at this hearing, we discussed an alternative answer: "I know lots of people I would not want as a neighbor." In that same spirit, one could make that answer more powerful, and say: "It's amazing how few people I would truly want as a neighbor, including many university faculty."

These answers, however, still buy into the question. Let us reconsider the evaluation issue, which was whether this girl had the possibility of successful treatment as a juvenile. The girl was not evaluated for her neighborliness. She was not evaluated for how well she fit into the small neighborhood in which Bob resides. Her assessment was aimed at the specific *Kent* criteria.

What answer could have addressed this difficulty? I suggest two possibilities: "I would not think for a second of offering an opinion as an expert on an issue outside the scope of my evaluation." "Her ability to behave responsibly as my personal neighbor were not addressed in my evaluation, nor

194

would they be addressed in the evaluations conducted by any clinical or child psychologist I know."

THE MAXIM: *When cross-examination demands move to you personally, seek to decline the gambit and stay with the objective and specific purposes of your findings.*

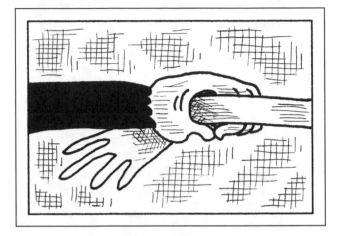

42

More Pulls to Extrapolate

"**D**O YOU THINK THIS YOUNG MAN WILL be able to go to his high school prom?" the expert was asked during cross-examination after she had testified about the results of her neuropsychological assessment of a teenager injured in an auto accident.

As in chapter 41, this question brings the expert into a realm in which the assessment appears to apply, but does not. The temptation is to answer yes or no, one way or another, based on judgments of social isolation, interpersonal skills or deficits, ability to be in crowds, panic attacks, and so forth. But the cross-examination question is not explicitly about those issues. After all, people can go to proms for a few minutes, they can attend and stay in a corner, they can be dragged by a friend, and they can go to a prom while in substantial psychological distress. Be careful not to extrapolate into an area about which one is not knowledgeable; in this case, it was about prom contexts, the social network around proms, and what the prom means to the evaluee.

It is possible that as an evaluator you might have, indeed, conducted an in-depth assessment of what the prom meant to this particular young man, examined its social context, and gathered third-party information related to the prom. In that case, a definitive answer is legitimate. In almost all cases, however, this specific an evaluation will not have been made. When the question of a prom (or other situation-specific actions) arises unexpectedly during a cross-examination and witnesses feel on the spot, they may be inclined to discuss readiness for the prom. This inclination is to be avoided.

What should witnesses do? The limits of knowledge and the boundaries of the evaluation should be stated clearly and strongly. One might respond: "I can address this young man's impairments and psychological functioning in more detail, if you would like. I have not assessed the nature of the prom at his high school, what it means to him, or what skills or levels of functioning it would take to be present at the prom, or to function adequately in that setting, or to have a good time. I have no opinion on whether he would be able to attend the prom."

The prom question is representative of a broad class of questions in which testifying experts are requested to discuss content related to their conclusions, but also go beyond what they actually know. This kind of effort to get experts to extrapolate is seductive when the question seeks to apply known and firm conclusions to a variety of social or occupational situations. The expert might be asked, as well, whether the evaluee can ever get a job as a programmer in a software firm. Even if the assessment revealed that the person cannot sustain concentration for more than a few minutes, that deficit does not mean that a job in computer programming could not be obtained. After all, jobs may be obtained for a variety of reasons, including family influence and bad personnel screening. Instead of saying no, the witness might wish to state that the person would not be likely to be able to produce well-developed programming code, assuming, of course, that the expert knows just what skills and abilities it takes to develop programming code. For most experts, the safest reply might be to assert that they are not familiar with the hiring practices and criteria for employment in software firms.

THE MAXIM: *When the cross-examining attorney seeks extrapolation of your findings and conclusions to specific situations, be careful not to go beyond the limits of what you have actually found and know.*

❦ 43 ❦

Echo Effects

DR. MARTIN WILLIAMS OF REDWOOD ESTATES, California wrote to me about a particular technique that attorneys have used in cross-examining him on the stand. He described it this way:

> Whatever you say during cross examination, no matter how damaging to the opposing attorneys' case, they repeat your comments, with gleeful emphasis, to make the jury believe you just said something very, very helpful to their case. I presume this tactic is predicated on the jury being so dumb that they react only to process and not to content, so that the juror will think: "I don't know what the hell that Dr. Williams just said, but the attorney was sure happy with it. I guess Dr. Williams really agrees with the opposing attorney after all."
>
> A good example was a case in which I was arguing, consistent with my publications, that not all therapists are required to keep the same boundaries, and that not all schools of therapy

agree on what the appropriate boundaries are. The plaintiff claimed that therapist–patient sex had taken place, an allegation that was vehemently denied. Since there was no independent corroboration of the allegations, the plaintiff was arguing that a host of boundary violations known to have occurred, strongly implied that sexual boundaries must have also been crossed.

Malpractice insurance excludes coverage for therapist–patient sex. Thus, the plaintiff was trying to show that "negligent treatment" had occurred, treatment that was harmful in and of itself, even if the alleged sex had not taken place. The crux of the negligent treatment was supposedly "boundary violations," and one of the most egregious of these was so-called "negligent self-disclosure." The plaintiff's expert had argued that excessive self-disclosure is detrimental to treatment and that it had harmed the plaintiff.

I countered the opinions of the plaintiff's expert by testifying, "Self-disclosure is not necessarily unethical and it can be perfectly legitimate and helpful." I was surprised to see a big smile spread across the face of the plaintiff's attorney. With great satisfaction, he repeated:

"So (with the syllable stretched out) self-disclosure can be perfectly legitimate and helpful."

Watching this attorney, an observer would have no idea that "negligent self-disclosure" was a central claim in his case. It was the last thing he wanted to hear from me. However, with a dramatic flair he reacted for the jury's benefit as if I had just said exactly the perfect thing to prove his point and help him win his case.

At the time though, I was amazed to watch it happen and had no idea what I could do about it. My understanding is that I can answer questions, but I have no right to hold forth regarding the demeanor of the opposing attorney.

> After all, I am merely a witness in court—not leading a process group with the attorney as my patient. My hope was that the jury would pay attention to the content and ignore this manipulative process. In this instance they did.

Having one's testimony echoed back with such tangible delight can be a distressing and disorienting experience. The attorney's statement of pleasure and affirmation did not sit well. A discrepancy can be seen between the literal context of the expert's statement and the contradictory way in which it is received. This is a clever reframing that can serve an attorney well in occasional use. After all, if an attorney were to flush, stammer, and become visibly distressed on the occasion of a witness's statement that seemed to undermine his or her case, the jury would know at an emotional level the import of the testimony.

The echo effect did not work in the case above. Witnesses need to appreciate that the court considers both text— what they say literally—and context— how it comes across and is received. Furthermore, remember that juries and the courts do use more than testimony in coming to decisions, including elements such as the requirements of the law.

What should the expert do when a statement is echoed back? I propose two approaches. First, assume that the echo contains an implied question, and answer it. In reply to: "So self-disclosure can be perfectly legitimate and helpful." The expert can equally confidently state: "That is *exactly* correct. You understand *precisely* what I meant."

The other option applies for less combative witnesses, those who can move into almost a meditative moment of acceptance. They can choose to say nothing at all, and with a movement in the direction of profound serenity allow the gambit to wash over and past them. They may appreciate that every interpretation of their statements does not have to be corrected. The witnesses' task is not to set the court straight. Certainly, it is not to challenge the emotional display and posturing of opposing counsel. Rather, it is to stay affirming within one's testimony, to focus on what one is doing and stay there, and permit the examination process to unfold.

THE MAXIM: *Misleading echoes of experts' statements during cross-examinations may be met actively with confident restatements or passively by comfortable acceptance of the normal examination process.*

❧ 44 ❧

Familiar Presentation of Famous Studies

THE CROSS-EXAMINATION WAS WELL UNDER WAY. The psychologist who was testifying had effortlessly turned aside the challenges to his methods and findings. Then, having run out of directly relevant questions, the attorney turned to topics that sought to discredit the psychological profession.

"Isn't it true," the attorney asked with earnest zeal, "that the research by David Rosenhan called *On Being Sane in Insane Places* raises into question the diagnostic accuracy of the mental health professions?"

This kind of question startles some expert witnesses. It is not unusual for witnesses to stumble and reply with hesitation and uncertainty, weakly defending their work against the background of studies that may point to contradictory findings of methods.

However, this witness replied, "Not at all. I was discussing this research with Dr. Rosenhan the other day, and neither he nor I see it as critical of careful, detailed, responsible, and systematic evaluations done by trained and experienced professionals."[20]

The attorney was stunned. She then challenged whether he had actually spoken to the same David Rosenhan whose studies are taught (and she had read about) in introductory psychology classes—he had—and whether mental health evaluations could at all be taken seriously—they could. She quickly left the topic.

Not many witnesses can draw on the coincidence of having talked to the well-known figures in their fields and, shortly afterward, being asked about them in court. Nevertheless, there are alternative reasonable ways of mobilizing just that kind of professional–personal familiarity when challenged in court.

One path is going to conferences or workshops to hear talks by well-known professionals. The same people whose work is cited in legal publications as a vehicle for attacking expert testimony are often regular and visible speakers at conventions and workshops. Furthermore, most of these people are open to talking after their presentations with colleagues who want to raise professional issues.

Most of these well-known people are generously responsive to e-mail inquiries. After I published a paper I had coauthored on the ethical confrontation of unethical colleagues (Brodsky & McKinzey, 2002), I received a series of e-mails from different persons requesting my comments about specific applications or problems related to the content of the

---

[20]Bruce Frumkin, personal communication, August 26, 2002, provided the details of a cross-examination that followed these questions and answers.

article. I did my best to write replies in proportion to the seriousness and depth of the inquiry, sometimes going on at considerable length. If any of these people were asked about these issues and my article on the stand, I would hope that they would have asserted that they had just been in touch with me and that here was what I wrote to them.

The personal contact has a powerful validating effect. The expert witness who uses it is neither a parrot nor reporter, but becomes something different—an individual who is personally linked with professional knowledge.

Sound professional or scholarly knowledge is almost as good. There is a special pleasure to hear an attorney ask a question directly drawn from an accepted source that you know and have mastered. It puts you in a position to interpret or critique the source. Attorneys often hope to ambush the witness by laying a trap built on something substantial. The well-prepared witness anticipates the traps by being well-read and exposed to the common and current foundations of knowledge.

THE MAXIM: *Read and know the essential scholarly resources in your field, listen to talks by these scholars, e-mail them with questions, and be prepared to rebut cross-examinations on these topics in personal–professional ways.*

❦ 45 ❦

Highly Paid, Well-Known Experts

Attorney:	How much are you being paid for your testimony?
Dr. Rosekrans:	(looking at clock) I think it will be about four hours, so I will bill for $320.00.
Judge:	That is $80 an hour.
Dr. Rosekrans:	That is correct.
Judge:	Dr. Leonore Walker charged $4,000 for an afternoon testifying.
Dr. Rosekrans:	I am retired and I don't do this for a living.

When Dr. Frank Rosekrans of Spokane sent me this excerpt from a trial in which he was testifying, my reaction was to consider three alternative ways in which he might have handled this situation. First, he might have explained that he was not being paid for his testimony or opinion, but only for his time. Paid expert witnesses make statements like this frequently to avoid any hint of being a bought witness. I am not convinced, however, that these assertions of integrity and time-not-opinions being purchased serve the aims that experts seek. To begin with, most experts when asked about fees make statements of this sort. Some witnesses make their rebuttals of the implications so strong that observers may well think they protest too much. These occasions call for mild responses and modest clarifications. After all, the occasional witnesses whose opinions might be compromised by fees are probably those persons who would most fiercely deny any such influences.

The second of Dr. Rosekrans's alternative choices might have been to wait (and hope) for the judge to ask the implied question before answering. Still, tone of voice surely can be a form of a request for a response, and witnesses should try to be responsive to judges.

Finally, and perhaps most important, he could have omitted the statement that he was retired and did not do this work to earn an income. Although honest, such a statement might have made his role appear more as a dilettante than as a committed professional.

The position in which this witness found himself was common, that is, testifying in a case in which a highly paid, well-known expert has been retained by opposing counsel. Witnesses in his situation frequently feel inadequate and concerned that they will look inept and be judged negatively because of the comparison. Research data suggest they need not necessarily be concerned.

One research report is particularly relevant. Cooper and Neuhaus (2000) noted that peripheral and heuristic cues, such as prestige and manner of speech, had been shown to increase credibility of expert testimony. They exposed mock jurors to audiotaped testimony in a simulated case in which the essential issue was whether exposure to PCBs had been the immediate cause of a plaintiff's cancer. In their scenarios, the high and low pay conditions had experts receiving $4,800 and $600, respectively, for their time in court. The highly credentialed expert had many publications and taught at a prestigious university in contrast to the fewer publications and more obscure institutional affiliation of the modestly credentialed expert. Pay and credentials by themselves made no difference. However, the expert with the combination of impressive credentials and high pay was markedly less effective as assessed by the jury verdict when compared to the lower paid, less credentialed expert. The jurors thought the high pay influenced the expert's opinion, if information suggested he or she was an expert for hire.

When the testimony was complex, jurors were especially skeptical and negative abut testimony by highly paid experts who made frequent court appearances. When the testimony was not complex, credentials, frequency of testimony, and pay made no difference. The lesson, of course, is not to speak over the heads of jurors, even about complex scientific issues.

One final finding relates to jurors' impressions of experts and their behaviors. Cooper and Neuhaus (2000) reported that "The more the expert was liked and the more credible he was perceived to be, the more convincing he was. The expert who was neither liked nor credible was not persuasive" (p. 168).

Typical expert witnesses like Frank Rosekrans do not have to feel inferior or intimidated about going against well-known experts. Caution may be in order more for experts who testify often for high fees. They should ensure they do not come across as imperious, that their behavior is positive and affable, and that they do not bury the jurors in scientific details. Those behaviors may backfire.

THE MAXIM: *Local expert witnesses of moderate credentials often are equal in persuasion or in complex cases may have an advantage over the big name expert.*
They should focus on what they know and have found, and try not to compare themselves to impressively credentialed persons who also testify.

❧ 46 ❧

Surprise Demands

THE YOUNG WOMAN STOOD NEXT TO Dr. Thomas Conboy, who was waiting for the courthouse elevator. She had been sitting in the front row during all of Dr. Conboy's testimony. From her emotional expressions, he had come to believe that she was related to the deceased victim. As they waited for the elevator, the woman caught Dr. Conboy's eye, and said: "It's a nice day outside, isn't it?"

Feeling cautious about speaking to possible participants or family members in this capital murder trial, but at the same time not wanting to be impolite, he responded, "Yes, it's a nice day." She looked him in the eye, and with a cutting tone of voice, said "You won't be seeing many of these once you are burning in hell with Satan. How dare you try to get off the man who murdered and mutilated my grandmother?"

Dr. Conboy did not say anything back, but looked away. As they waited for the elevator and then took it down to the ground floor, she continued to harangue him with accusations of being in bed with Satan and being a disgrace to the human race. He remained silent and averted her gaze.

What Dr. Conboy did was exactly right. There is no point to an expert engaging in a discussion of this sort with a family member. As awkward as it may seem to accept such accusations silently, there are few other acceptable alternatives. Still, two other possibilities are worth noting.

One possibility is to walk away. You can walk anywhere, down the corridor, to the rest rooms, to the witness room if it is still available, or to a staircase. One has no obligation to stay in such a situation.

A second possibility requires that you ascertain that the accuser is not another witness. Witnesses are supposed to form opinions and act independently of each other. If so, then one might say: "What a horrible loss" or "There is no way someone can have a grandmother killed without feeling devastated" or "How awful this must be for you."

These options are not intended to soothe the relative. Rather, they are intended to make the expert feel better, by moving from the necessarily detached and objective courtroom role to a sympathetic role more fitting to talking with a grieving person. Do not talk about Satan, do not explain your role as an expert witness, and do not address any aspect of the case. Instead, move to a broken record repetition of expressing sympathy.

What if the woman continued to accuse you of being an instrument of the devil, despite the statements of sympathy? In that instance, you could excuse yourself and quickly leave. Do not stay in such conversations. One way to be in personal control is to get out of there.

Later on in the same trial, Tom Conboy was confronted with an interesting question. He had testified that the accused murderer had suffered brain injuries in the several months

211

before the killing as a result of closed head injuries from a motor vehicle accident, a subsequent stroke, and considerable alcohol and drug abuse. He described the defendant as substantially impaired in his ability to process information accurately and well, and suffering from limitations in cognitive abilities, memory, judgment, and perception. Then the prosecuting attorney asked this question:

> Doctor, assume hypothetically that before the killing the defendant had made a statement heard by a witness that he could kill anyone and get away with it because he had been diagnosed with brain damage. Wouldn't that statement be consistent with someone who knew what he was doing and was able to judge the consequences of his criminal actions?

In this situation, the common experience of the expert is to think "Oh no, I have been backed into a corner." One constructive way to think about this is to stay faithful to the nature of your evaluation. After all, you have not heard or assessed the quality of information contained in this hypothetical. Who was the observer? Exactly what did the defendant say? In what context was it said? Statements taken out of context may be restated or presented in court by an attorney who has a motive to emphasize or excerpt certain parts. As a consequence, such statements should always be viewed with a skeptical attitude.

Two possible responses follow: "No. Based on my evaluation, the defendant is not capable of carrying out complex actions that require advance planning, forethought, and accurate comprehension of the consequences." Or: "It is certainly possible he could have made such a statement or repeated such a statement that someone else made about him. In my best professional judgment he was not rationally and knowledgeably able to develop or carry out such a plan."

The Maxim: *Do not permit interested parties or attorneys to coerce you into accepting interactions or assertions that are inconsistent with your expert role or findings.*

■ ■ ■ ■ ■ ■ ■ ■ ■ ■ ■ ■ ■ ■ ■

CLARITY AND FOCUS

The Tough and Tangential Cross-Examination

T HE ADMINISTRATIVE HEARING IN FEDERAL COURT had started with evidence of alleged verbal abuse of the residents of a nursing home. It ended with apparently relevant questions, which were actually non sequiturs, asked of the key expert witness. The undisputed part of the story was that elderly residents had been told repeatedly by the staff that they were worthless, inept, and unsanitary. The milder statements on the record included staff members saying to the residents: "You stink." "You're not nice." "You're no good."

The large corporation that ran this and many other nursing homes eventually found itself in court for an administrative hearing about verbal abuse after the responsible federal agency had withheld reimbursement payments. The sole expert retained by the government to testify in this case was an experienced scholar and consultant who had been studying nursing homes for 20 years. She was asked to offer opinions about whether the statements listed above had taken place and whether they were abusive. She was not asked to interview the nursing home residents, but rather to draw conclusions from thousands of progress notes that she had sorted and abstracted, from reports of inspectors who monitored the nursing home, and from standardized reporting data from the nursing home.

When the expert was retained, she made it clear to the attorneys for the government that she was not an expert in abuse. Her areas of expertise were in staffing and operation of nursing homes, and in the quality and content of mandated inspection reports about nursing homes. However, it was her first time in court, and her testimony in court did not progress as she expected.

The direct examination lasted 5 minutes. The attorneys were young, new to their positions, and inexperienced. After credentialing the expert, just two questions were asked during direct:

Q. Do you think these residents are capable of giving accurate reports?
A. Yes, because there were two independent inspections that drew this conclusion, and because well-validated reporting data also pointed to this conclusion.
Q. Do statements, like "you're no good" constitute verbal abuse?
A. Yes, based on examples from congressional hearings and from government reports related to the governing statute.

The questioning became hard and increasingly tangential during the cross.

Q. Do you have the Form 406 there?
A. I don't know.

She stated that she had many progress notes and many inspection reports. She shuffled and searched through the stacks of files and papers she had brought to the stand, searching for Form 406. The question about Form 406 seemed disconnected from anything said during direct. The difficulty in finding this form unsettled her and left this normally composed gerontologist unsettled and shaken. What should she have done? She should have immediately replied: "I don't know. I don't use the numbers of the forms to organize and keep track of them." Then a series of questions were asked to which the expert gave rapid identical responses:

Q. Have you ever met these residents of the nursing home who claim they have been abused?
A. No.
Q. Did you do additional assessments yourself beyond looking at what was in the records?
A. No.
Q. Did you talk with any of the staff?
A. No.

By this time the expert was feeling trapped and miserable. She might have made these negative assertions in response to these questions: "No, that's not what I do." "That was outside the boundaries of my evaluation."

Then the cross-examining attorney asked several questions that made the expert feel that she was coming across as picky and unrealistic.

Q. Would a statement like this be verbal abuse? "You dirtied yourself?"
A. Yes, according to the congressional panel that set up this statute.
Q. Isn't it true that these statements are not even written anywhere? That you had to go to the web and hunt them up, didn't you?
A. (Meekly) Yes.

218

At the point in the cross, the witness needed to be assertive, not passively accepting the tangential assumption of the attorney that she had to be personally responsible for the information she utilized. She might have responded: "Although the specific examples may be discussed at length, the overriding principles and governing rules are clear, explicit, and exactly on target in identifying the variety of ways in which nursing home residents can be abused!"

Finally, the cross-examining attorney, having sensed pay dirt, closed with questions that further pursued the expert's acknowledgment that she had not personally assessed the credibility of the abused residents.

Q. Are you aware that Mrs. D. was found on December 1st of last year to have lied about somebody stealing her clothes?

A. No.

Q. Would that have been a significant factor to consider in reaching your conclusion?

A. Yes.

The expert gave in when she should have resisted. The first question was drawn on information to which the expert was not privy. Experts should never assume that such information embedded in cross-examination questions is accurate. For example, Mrs. D. may have been accused of the theft of clothing by an unreliable or confused fellow resident. Mrs. D. may have been one of several people who were investigated about stealing clothes. Instead of the simple yes, the expert might have said:

> I had no knowledge at the time I reviewed the documents and I have no knowledge now that Mrs. D. has actually been stealing anything. However, even if Mrs. D. has stolen something, that in no way rules out or contradicts the multiple sources of information in my review of the data that point to her having been a victim of abuse.

219

This administrative hearing was before an unsympathetic judge, who felt that if the abuse was not physical abuse, it was a minor infraction not worth the court's time. This expert had been impressive in a number of settings not only by her depth of knowledge but also her poise. However, in this court situation, she was insufficiently prepared by inexperienced attorneys, and then uncharacteristically gave in or rattled on. What should she have done?

- Breathed deeply.
- Slowed down.
- Taken time to think through the implicit assumptions in the questions.
- Attended carefully to the non sequiturs in which the questions did not clearly follow the statements of method and findings.
- Assertively restated the methods and findings and opinions as she saw them.

THE MAXIM: *Even poised and knowledgeable professionals can be muddled and ineffective on the stand. During cross-examinations, think through the actual connections between your findings and the questions asked during cross. Answer in terms that are meaningful for your conclusions.*

❧ 48 ❧

Data Errors

"**M**AY I APPROACH THE WITNESS?" the attorney asked, and the predictable response from the bench was affirmative. The attorney walked immediately in front of me and asked if I had a copy of the MMPI-2 profile I had described. No, I did not. She looked through her papers, and she had no copy. Finally, the attorney who had retained me came up with a copy. Brandishing it prominently in her hand, she held it up to me to examine, and began to ask about my prior description of the results during the earlier direct examination.

Then I looked at the profile that I had seen at least a dozen times before. Four high points, all well-elevated between T = 80 and T = 83, were present, but not including the scale that assesses depression. It was normal. I had just explained and interpreted a pattern of four high points, using a large visual display. I had discussed the evaluee's depression, which was manifested in part on the MMPI-2 and illustrated in the transparency by a high score on depression.

My first thoughts were: How could this happen? Had I made an unconscious error? Had I copied the information incorrectly? Had I looked at the separate Content Scale for Depression, which was very high, and confused it?

I knew I was wrong. I had committed an error that could stand out from everything else I had said during 5 hours on the stand. After all, if I incorrectly copied and reported one piece of important information, everything else I reported could be suspect.

This kind of situation is preventable. In fact, I thought I had engaged in prevention by reviewing my records several times, going over the findings with the retaining attorney, using my dependable test scoring company, and having a graduate student join me and discuss my report. I went back afterward to see whether I could trace the sequence or moment at which I slipped. The correct results and profile were exactly as handed to me during cross-examination. The results were incorrectly copied onto the sheet used for the transparency.

How does one handle such an obvious error in presenting data? Immediate and open admission of responsibility is the only possibility. "I am embarrassed," I said, feeling just that. "I copied it incorrectly. The one you just showed me is the right one."

Then she leaped at my exposed fault. "Therefore, your conclusions about depression are not right, isn't that so?" I spoke briefly to the content scale of the MMPI—which I checked later, and it was right—and then indicated that no one test scale had led to my diagnosis. Rather, I explained, the conclusion was seated in the whole evaluation results. But my normally strong and confident tone of voice was subdued and my words caught a little in my throat. During redirect, the damage was reasonably repaired, but not enough to salve the severity of my self-criticisms.

THE MAXIM: *Data errors can creep into testimony in many forms. One cannot be too compulsive in checking one's basic data.*

❦ 49 ❦

Cross-Examinations
About Tests

THE CRITICAL EXAMINATION OF PSYCHOLOGICAL TESTS for acceptability in the courts seems to come and go in waves.
During 1999 and 2000 the test on the examination table
was the Millon Clinical Multiaxial Inventory (MCMI), an
examination process that reflects its increasing use by
psychologists. Well-prepared attorneys often begin their
cross-examinations about psychological examinations by asking about desirable characteristics of scientifically sound
tests. From that point, they seek to contrast the elements
of good scientific tests with the test under critical examination. This approach to cross-examination has been applied
to all tests.

The following cross-examination questions have been
constructed in specific response to the debate in the literature
about the MCMI.

Q1. What makes a good psychological test?

Q2. Why do researchers use meta-analyses to study the worth of psychological tests?

Q3. What are effect sizes?

To these three questions, the answers are straightforward. Psychologist witnesses do not have to be defensive. Rather, they should answer Q1 with comments about the nature of reliability and validity, Q2 with the desirability of putting together findings from many studies in a meaningful scientific context, and Q3 by discussing the nature of effect sizes as an indicator of the power of results. Now we move to more challenging questions.

Q4. Are you familiar with the 1999 *Law and Human Behavior* article by Rogers, Salekin, and Sewell that questioned whether the MCMI meets the Daubert standard?

Only two responses are appropriate here: either the witness is familiar with the article or is not. One does not have to be embarrassed about not knowing any single study, because there is a flood of journal articles and books in psychological knowledge. The following question assumes the witness has said that he or she is not familiar with the article.

Q5. Would you be surprised to learn that they reported that their meta-analysis of 33 studies failed to establish adequate validity for the MCMI?

Some witnesses may accurately answer that they would be surprised at such a negative finding about a test they value. My preferred and truthful answer to all such surprise questions (a common tactic in cross-examination) is that no findings in any journal surprise me, because I am aware of how any study is always seated in particular hypotheses, methodology, and analyses that may be questioned.

Q6. Please read aloud to the court the underlined passage.

This request is not a question. Nevertheless, it is an accepted means of introducing substantial content with which to question a witness.

> Only 2 of the 14 (MCMI) scales evidenced even marginal convergent validity. (p. 431)
> While the MCMI-II offers useful data on three Axis II disorders, its applicability to forensic issues remains virtually untested. Many of the forensic issues (e.g., sanity) have not been systematically evaluated with the MCMI-II. Therefore, the MCMI cannot be employed to address issues of legal standards. (p. 439)

Assume now that the attorney follows up this witness recitation with a series of questions designed to elicit further admissions about the problematic quality of this test in forensic settings. Here are some possible responses:

1. The MCMI is a widely accepted and used test. (This response addresses the acceptance component of admission of expert methodology, but it does not address reliability or validity concerns.)

2. Much vigorous disagreement exists about methods in meta-analyses. (This answer is a judgment call. One expert I checked with said that there is agreement about the method. Another asserted that some aspects of meta-analysis are indeed disputed.)

3. Tests are used to develop hypotheses rather than to answer questions. (I like this answer because it is exactly how I see the use of tests for the courts.)

4. The 1997 second edition of the MCMI-III manual answers many questions about the test. (The 1997 manual is indeed improved. One of the authors of the critical article has argued to me that two of the major shortcomings in the manual are criterion contamination and accepting subclinical elevations in scales as "hits." The response, however, is accurate. Many questions are answered.)

226

5. The August 2000 issue of *Law and Human Behavior* published two scholarly rebuttals to the Rogers et al. article. (In order to give this response, the witness should be familiar with the specifics of the rebuttals and the reply by Rogers et al. [2000] to the rebuttals.)

6. In general, admit weaknesses of the MCMI for forensic purposes while reporting why it was chosen for the present task. (It is unbecoming to defend any test and certainly the MCMI as beyond criticism. At the same time, one should be able to recreate for the court how one made the decision to use it.)

A new version of the MCMI is available, the MCMI-III.[21] When I discussed this new version with my colleague Randy Salekin (who coauthored the critical article), Randy was clear and convinced that the MCMI in its various forms should not be used for forensic purposes. On my part, I see the choice of specific methods for forensic purposes as beyond the scope of this book. Instead, I would encourage witnesses to choose their methods with care and based on good information in the literature. Once methods are chosen, witnesses should use that information in both direct and cross-examinations and be prepared to discuss the detailed issues that may be raised during cross.

THE MAXIM: *Good testimony starts with good methods. Expert witnesses should be prepared to discuss criticisms in the literature of their methods in a manner that is knowledgeable, candid, and contextual.*

---

[21] See http://assessments.ncspearson.com/assessments/tests/mcmi_3.htm.

❧ 50 ❧

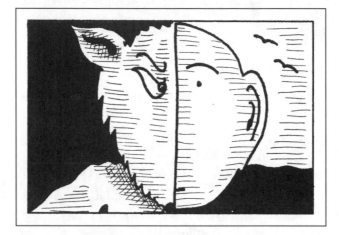

Sexual Predator
Testimony 1: Principles

TESTIFYING ABOUT OFFENDER RISK and future violence is not new for mental health professionals. At least since the era of indeterminate sentencing and the Patuxent, Maryland, treatment prison managed by psychological personnel, professionals have been asked or required to report to the courts whether convicted offenders are "dangerous." Accounts of this tormented process in the 1960s and 1970s can be seen in books of the era: *Psychologists in the Criminal Justice System* (Brodsky, 1973) and *The Right to Be Different* (Kittrie, 1971).

Wendy Weiss offered helpful feedback on a draft of this chapter.

The prediction of violence resurfaced in many ways in the 1990s. Following the rape and murder of 7-year-old Megan Kanka in 1994 by a twice-convicted sex offender, federal and state legislation resulted in every state having a version of Megan's Law requiring community notification of released sex offenders. Many states enacted a sexually violent predator law that allows convicted violent sex offenders to be kept past their sentences in prison or psychiatric hospitals, or to be identified for life as sexual predators, with various consequences. As a result, mental health professionals in many states now find themselves being called to testify about future sexual violence (Hoberman, 1999). In some states a likelihood of greater than 50% is the cut-off point at which experts may indicate that sexual violence is likely.

The Sexually Violent Predator statute in Pennsylvania (section 9795.4) is a representative example. A Sexual Offenders Assessment Board was instituted and the statute "requires the board member assigned to the court order to form an opinion if the offender meets the criteria set forth for Sexually Violent Predator." The statute defines a sexually violent predator as a person who has been convicted of a sexually violent offense " . . . and who is determined to be a sexually violent predator . . . due to a mental abnormality or personality disorder that makes the person likely to engage in predatory sexually violent offenses." When professionals give presentence testimony under this statute or similar ones about their assessments of sex offenders, they often are subjected to vigorous cross-examinations. Here are common scenarios in cross-examinations.

This first question is a lead-in.

"You have testified that Mr. White suffers from a mental abnormality or personality disorder that makes him likely to engage in predatory sexually violent offenses, is that correct?" (Yes)

Q1. To what specific degree of consistency and accuracy can mental health professionals (MHP) determine whether a person suffers from a mental abnormality? A personality disorder?

Q2. Isn't it true that what one MHP might call a disorder, another equally qualified MHP might well find to be within the range of ordinary and not abnormal behaviors?

Q3. You have testified as to mental abnormality. Isn't it accurate to say that the term *mental abnormality* has not been used in official and professional diagnostic manuals in your field for decades?

These first three questions address diagnosis. Q1 and Q2 are answered by noting that consistency depends on how carefully standardized procedures are followed in interviewing and assessment. Having specific reliability data in hand would help.

Q3 is intended to elicit discomfort and to put the expert on the defensive. This type of question may be worth taking a minute to consider the answer. One possible answer is "Yes, long ago we discarded the term, and I use it today only because it is part of the statute. The reason I go into detail about Mr. Johnson's actual DSM diagnosis and psychopathology is precisely because we do not use the legal terminology in our work."

Q4. You have testified that Mr. White is *likely* to engage in predatory sexually violent offenses. Let us discuss the term *likely*. Is the term *likely* part of normal and customary mental health nomenclature?

Suggested answer: Just as with the use of thousands of other ordinary words, such as *often, frequent,* and *apparent*, psychiatry does not consider that it has special ownership of ordinary words such as *likely*.

Q5.   At what percentage of likelihood do you determine that someone is truly likely to engage in a violent behavior? Would a 10% likelihood be enough to be likely? Would a 25% likelihood be enough to be likely? Would a 40% likelihood be enough to be likely? Would a 51% likelihood be enough to be likely? Would a 75% likelihood be enough to be likely? Is 100% likelihood necessary?

Note the word *truly* in the question. That word can distract the witness. If behavior is being assessed as likely, one can assume that it is the equivalent of truly likely. After all, the alternative is falsely likely or some unacceptable equivocal descriptor, such as probably likely.

Apart from the word *truly* in the question, this is not an unfair question. For many experts, it is useful to have thought the issue through in advance and to be prepared to answer. A helpful reply is that this is a professional judgment and that one has no specific number to attach to likelihood.

Q6a.   When one predicts behavior, it always has to be within some time frame, doesn't it? (Yes.)

Q6b.   Doesn't the social science literature indicate that the farther away in time one makes a prediction of behavior, the poorer you are at prediction? (Yes.)

Q6c.   Please indicate to the court in which of the following time periods you are most sure of your prediction of future sexual offending? In the next day. In the next week. In the next month. In the next year. In the next 5 years. In the next 10 years. In the next 20 years. In the next 40 years. Please indicate to the court in which of the following time periods you are least sure of your prediction of future sexual offending? In the next day. In the next week. In the next month. In the next year. In the next 5 years. In the next 10 years. In the next 20 years. In the next 40 years.

Answers to these questions are best presented in the context of the procedures used in prediction. If actuarial data and methods are used, specific estimates may be offered. If the judgment comes from assessment of offender behaviors without actuarial tables, the witness would be wise to decline the request, and explain that no exact time is specified in the predictive process. At the same time, such questions may serve as an impetus for witnesses to consider integrating actuarial foundations, a topic we consider shortly.

THE MAXIM: *Be prepared for challenges to basic concepts and accuracy by mobilizing relevant data and by acknowledging the context and limitations of your conclusions.*

❦ 51 ❦

Sexual Predator Testimony 2: Challenges to the Construct

I ROUTINELY BUT FUTILELY ASK FOR SAMPLE REPORTS to the court when I speak to professional groups about court testimony, so it was a pleasant surprise arriving at the airport when my host from the state organization of assessors of sexual predators handed me two reports. One was an evaluation of a man who had committed a sexual assault. It described the details of the assault in vivid and repetitive detail, and elaborated how the offender's diagnosis, history, age, offense, motivation, victims, and predatory behavior met each element of the state sexual predator statute.

Michelle E. Barnett offered helpful comments on an early draft of this chapter.

The second report was the subject of considerable discussion at the workshop. A distinguished forensic psychiatrist in the region had been retained by the defense and had written a report asserting that the defendant did not meet the criteria for being a sexual predator under the statute. In one part of the report, the psychiatrist noted that the statute defined predatory, in part, as establishing a relationship with the victim for the purpose of victimizing or assaulting her. Although the facts of the rape were uncontested, this psychiatrist concluded that the relationship had not been promoted for this purpose. To the workshop participants, the most disturbing parts of his report were his attacks on the statute itself. The participants often stumbled and had considerable difficulty when asked to respond to his and similar criticisms during their simulated testimony. These criticisms were:

1. The construct of sexually violent predator is not accepted clinically or scientifically.

2. No methodology can predict with reasonable clinical certainty whether individuals will sexually reoffend in the future. Mental health professionals cannot successfully make such predictions.

3. Long-term predictions are particularly uncertain because of the many uncertainties in future situations in which offenders may find themselves, and because of the general lessening of predictive accuracy over long periods of time.

For me, as well, the challenge to the construct was most interesting. Because of the ways in which sexual predator statutes and assessments have evolved, evaluators often find themselves testifying to the ultimate legal issue of whether an individual is a sexually violent predator. Schopp and Sturgis (1995) have pointed out that sexual predator statutes often fail to provide meaningful criteria and are not founded on sound conceptualizations of legal mental illness. The evaluators are then in a position of having to defend the notion of sexual predators as clinical entities, when, in fact, talking of "persistent and repeat violent sex offenders" is just as useful without the baggage of the word *predator*.

I advised the evaluators in this workshop to back off from describing anyone as a sexual predator, and, instead, to draw conclusions that stay close to their psychological data. Their reports to the court and their testimony could stay simply tied to diagnosis, assessment of violence history, and other components that make up the legal definition. When challenged about whether the statute and the construct of sexual predator are scientifically accepted, witnesses might choose to answer:

> The definition of sexually violent predator was a legislative and legal decision, not a scientific or clinical decision. The accuracy and appropriateness of legislative definitions and legal definitions are outside my area of expertise. I can only speak to the psychological nature of the man I assessed and aspects of his life, history, and offense.

Once experts state that an area is outside the boundaries of their expertise, a powerful coolant settles over the otherwise heated proceedings and the line of inquiry typically ceases. Retaining counsel and the judge become alerted, objections arise, and the court stops further questions. Good expert witnesses listen with care to questions that seem to reach beyond their special knowledge and actively speak up this way to avoid testifying about content in which they do not have expertise.

The related question of whether clinicians or other experts can predict violence surely would have received agreement at an earlier time that clinicians are inept. It had been a long-accepted finding that mental health professionals are poor predictors of violence, commonly overpredicting violence, in part because of the differential consequences to the

235

predictor. But things have changed. A series of promising actuarial instruments have been developed—for violence prediction in general and sex offending in particular—and it is fair to say that a vigorous scholarly debate now exists about their use. Some of the reviews of such instruments include reports of acceptable predictions (Grann, Belfrage, & Tengstrom, 2000), and acceptable reliability (Schopp, Scalora, & Pearce, 1999), whereas other reports have not supported contextualized predictions of violence (Skeem, Mulvey, & Lidz, 2000) and have challenged risk assessment assumptions by forensic practitioners (Rogers, 2000).

An additional issue that experts are asked to address is the limitation in long-term predictions as contexts change. My suggestion is that experts do not present themselves as certain. Behavior is a function of context and the farther away in time and place about which one makes predictions, the less certain one can be. Thus expert witnesses might reply to such challenges with the following:

> Of course, context affects behavior. And of course, all of us are much better at predicting behavior that may occur this month and this year than behaviors that may occur 20 years from now. These are always limiting factors. Based on the best information I have and the results of my assessment, and considering all of these limitations, it is my best professional judgment that Mr. J is (or is not) prone to repeating the violent and sexual acts for which he has been convicted in the past and present.

These assessment and testimony tasks are not easy, and the research literature is expanding rapidly. Practitioners often find it difficult to find time to do what they must in such predictive tasks, which is to keep up with methodologies and data relating to their work. In the meantime, they should keep their work and testimony within manageable limits and make explicit what they do and do not know.

236

THE MAXIM: *Testify about psychological, not legislative or legal constructs, and integrate research and knowledge into carefully delineated predictions.*

❧ 52 ❧

Actuarial Testimony

THE WAIL FROM ACADEMIC CIRCLES for actuarial rather than clinical predictions of human behavior has been heard for at least 40 years (Marchese, 1992; Meehl, 1954). The argument for actuarial prediction has been that it is unfailingly more accurate and accountable than every form of clinical prediction. In turn, the sometimes fierce, sometimes faltering, response from clinicians has been that actuarial research uses simplified concepts that do a disservice to the rich diversity of human experience and clinical expertise (Quinsey, Harris, Rice, & Cormier, 1998). After a slow, evolutionary process, actuarial and baseline predictions have become common, and sometimes accepted and used by clinicians. In forensic settings, the Federal Rules of Evidence have aided this acceptance, with their relatively recent emphasis on scientific methodology rather than general acceptability (Douglas, Cox, & Webster, 1999; Webster & Cox, 1997).

The criticisms that clinicians have traditionally made of actuarial assessments have now woven their way into the fabric of cross-examination of mental health and medical experts on sexual offending. Thus, the questions that follow are sometimes asked of witnesses who testify about sexual predator and aggressor issues:

Q1. Is it more accurate to say that comprehensiveness is essential or just very important in evaluating sex offender risk?

Q2. Doctor, isn't it unethical for an evaluator to ignore relevant data?

Q3. Isn't it true that currently available actuarial instruments do not and cannot consider all relevant aspects of any single individual?

Q1 is designed to get the witness to focus on notions of what is essential versus what is important, instead of the nature of a comprehensive evaluation. One way to think of it is that no evaluation is fully comprehensive, in the sense of knowing, studying, and assessing every aspect of the subject's life. Evaluations are always selective and representative. The real issue is ensuring that the methods give an accurate portrayal, not that they assess everything.

Q2 is similar in the sense that there is a powerful pull for the witness to agree. Indeed, we could make the case that it is not at all unethical to ignore relevant data. I am not certain what ethical codes address this issue. After all, much relevant data can be intentionally ignored, as long as other data that tap into the same domain of functioning are utilized. I suggest a simple no to Q2.

Q3 calls for a restatement of what actuarial instruments do. Of course, they do not consider all relevant aspects. A good answer might be, "Absolutely. That is exactly true."

These next questions are intended to challenge the generalization of actuarial databases.

Q4. Doctor, do you agree that it is the habitual course of criminal sexual conduct by the person in question which is the basis for predicting danger to the public, not the course of misconduct committed by other persons?

Q5.   Don't your so-called actuarial statistics come from the violent behavior of persons other than Mr. Johnson? And isn't it fair to say that your results are based on statistical evidence regarding the behavior of other people?

Q4 may make the witness feel unnecessarily defensive. It surely is the immediate subject whose record is at issue. The twist is in Q5. In reply, consider pointing out the use of comparative statistics in which Mr. Johnson was viewed with regard to the people in the database. This may be a good opportunity to assert that your role is never to confine anyone, but simply seek to provide a scientific foundation for conclusions that are made by others about future violence.

Challenges to clinical judgment are the opposite of actuarial challenges. Experts who have not used baseline data (of course, one can argue that all standardized tests draw in part on baseline data) can be questioned at length. They might be asked if they relied in part on clinical judgment or gut feeling. One can then reply by speaking of using structured assessments within clinical judgment in coming to conclusions.

Q6.   Are error rates important in predicting future behaviors of sex offenders? Tell us doctor, what are the error rates for the actuarial method? And what are your own error rates when you use this method?[22]

These questions are answered from knowledge of the literature. Often cross-examining attorneys will have taken questions of this sort verbatim from an academic article or from a consultant. Once witnesses show that they can discuss

---

[22]Some of these questions were suggested by Dr. Faulder Colby.

error rates knowledgeably, attorneys move to other topics with lightning speed. Being able to cite one study with one meaningful set of error rates and true positive rates is usually all it takes.

Other related questions often emerge from the scientific literature. Thus, a prepared cross-examining attorney may ask the following questions about hindsight bias:

Q7. Doctor, what is hindsight bias? What form does it take in psychology?

Q8. Are evaluators who use hindsight bias aware that they are using it? When aren't they aware of it? Can you assure this court, based on scientific information, that hindsight bias has not influenced your judgment?

Q7 opens the door to the knowledgeable witness who should run with it, explaining the issue in depth and how awareness of possible hindsight bias can help inoculate assessors from its effects. The last part of Q8, assuring the court that hindsight bias has not affected one's judgment, is tougher. If one answers yes, then scientific proof may be requested, a proof that may not be forthcoming. If one is unable to offer reassurance, then it is an admission of possible subjectivity and contamination. One reply is for the witness to explain that scientific findings generalize, and that this case is representative of the study samples.

An attorney may then come forward with a question that seems relevant but is actually a non sequitur (and should be answered as such):

Q9. Do you have any research foundation, even one study, that indicates that you psychologists are any better at predicting dangerousness than are lay people?

Q10. Isn't it an accepted standard that there is no known set of personality characteristics that can differentiate the sexual abuser from the nonabuser?

Q11.   Isn't it accepted that psychological profiles cannot be used to prove or disprove an individual's propensity to act in a sexually violent manner? And, doctor, doesn't that apply exactly to you, as well?

These questions fall into the genre of questions that experts should explain, discuss, and affirm in the context of what the actuarial predictions do. If explanatory opportunities do not exist, experts should strongly and positively agree, without worrying about explaining further.

THE MAXIM: *Testimony about actuarial applications calls for being comfortably seated in the context, strengths, and weaknesses of such data.*

242

References

Abagnale, F. W. (1980). *Catch me if you can.* New York: Broadway.

Appelbaum, P. S. (1984). Confidentiality in the forensic evaluation. *International Journal of Law and Psychiatry, 7,* 285–300.

Asimov, I. (1975). *100 original lecherous limericks.* New York: Walker.

Banks, I. A. (2000). *Look to windward.* New York: Pocket.

Boccaccini, M. T. (2002). What do we really know about witness preparation? *Behavioral Sciences and the Law, 20,* 161–189.

Boccaccini, M. T. (2003). Impact of witness preparation training on the use of targeted testimony delivery skills, perceived credibility, and evaluations of guilt. (Doctoral dissertation, University of Alabama, 2003).

Boccaccini, M. T., & Brodsky, S. L. (1999). Diagnostic test usage by forensic psychologists in emotional injury cases. *Professional Psychology, 30,* 253–259.

Boccaccini, M. T., & Brodsky, S. L. (2002). Believability of expert and lay witnesses: Implications for trial consultation. *Professional Psychology: Research and Practice, 33,* 384–388.

Brodsky, S. L. (1964). Self-disclosure in dormitory residents who seek counseling. *Psychology, 1*(3), 12–14.

Brodsky, S. L. (1971). A touch of sanity. *Worm Runners Digest, 12,* 99–100.

Brodsky, S. L. (1972). The quiet passing of Nough Pennix. *Worm Runners Digest, 14,* 52.

Brodsky, S. L. (1973). *Psychologists in the criminal justice system.* Champaign–Urbana: University of Illinois Press.

Brodsky, S. L. (1982). Prison class action suits: The aftermaths. In J. Gunn & D. P. Farrington (Eds.), *Abnormal offenders, delinquency, and the criminal justice system* (pp. 61–76). Chichester, England: Wiley.

Brodsky, S. L. (1993). The private sharing of professional self. *Voices: The Art and Science of Psychotherapy, 29*(2), 50–54.

Brodsky, S. L. (1999). *The expert expert witness: More maxims and guidelines for testifying in court.* Washington, DC: American Psychological Association.

Brodsky, S. L. (2002, March). *Competency to be executed: The death qualified expert. Capital Case Litigation Mini Conference.* Paper presented at the biennial meeting of the American Psychology-Law Society, Austin, TX.

Brodsky, S. L., & McKinzey, R. K. (2002). The ethical confrontation of the unethical forensic colleague. *Professional Psychology: Research and Practice, 33*, 307–309.

Brodsky, S. L., Zapf, P. A., & Boccaccini, M. T. (2001). The last competency: An examination of legal, ethical, and professional ambiguities regarding evaluations of competency for execution. *Journal of Forensic Psychology Practice, 1*(2), 1–25.

Butcher, J. N., Dahlstrom, W. G., Graham, J. R., Tellegen, A., & Kaemmer, B. (1989). *Minnesota Multiphasic Personality Inventory—2nd Edition: Manual for administration and scoring*. Minneapolis: University of Minnesota Press.

Cannon, D. E. (2001). *Effects of ingratiation during attorney-conducted voir dire*. Unpublished master's thesis, University of Alabama, Tuscaloosa.

Capote, T. (1965). *In cold blood: A true account of a multiple murder and its consequences*. New York: Random House.

Card, O. S. (2002). *Shadow puppets*. New York: Tor.

Carpenter, R. H. (1990). The statistical profile of language behavior with Machiavellian intent or while experiencing caution and avoiding self-incrimination. In R. W. Rieber & W. A. Stewart (Eds.), *Annals of the New York Academy of Sciences: Vol. 606*. The Language Scientist as Expert in the Legal Setting: Issues in Forensic Linguistics (pp. 5–17). New York: New York Academy of Sciences.

Cooper, J., & Neuhaus, I. M. (2000). The "hired gun" effect: Assessing the effect of pay, frequency of testifying, and credentials on the perception of expert testimony. *Law and Human Behavior, 24*, 149–172.

Craig, W., & Pepler, D. J. (1997). Observations of bullying and victimization in the schoolyard. *Canadian Journal of School Psychology, 2*, 41–60.

Craig, W. M., Pepler, D. J., & Atlas, R. (2000). Observations of bullying on the playground and in the classroom. *International Journal of School Psychology, 21*, 22–36.

Davis, D. L., & Brodsky, S. L. (1992). Psychotherapy with the unwilling client. *Residential Treatment for Children and Youth, 9*(3), 15–27.

Douglas, K. S., Cox, D. N., & Webster, C. D. (1999). Violence risk assessment: Science and practice. *Legal and Criminological Psychology, 4*, 149–184.

Eastwood, C. (2002). *Child sex complaints in the criminal justice system*. Queensland University of Technology, School of Learning and Professional Studies, Brisbane, Australia.

Everington, C., & Luckasson, R. (1992). *Competence assessment for standing trial for defendants with mental retardation: Test manual*. Worthington, OH: IDS.

Gaiman, N. (1999). *Stardust*. New York: Avon.

Giles, H., & Williams, A. (1992). Accommodating hypercorrection: A communication model. *Language and Communication, 12*, 343–356.

244

Godinez v. Moran, 509 U.S. 389 (1993).

Grann, M., Belfrage, H., & Tengstrom, A. (2000). Actuarial assessment of risk for violence: Predictive validity of the VRAG and the historical part of the HRC-20. *Criminal Justice and Behavior, 27,* 97–114.

Greenberg, S. A., & Shuman, D. W. (1997). Irreconcilable conflict between therapeutic and forensic roles. *Professional Psychology: Research and Practice. 28,* 50–55.

Grisso, T. (1990). Forensic evaluations and the fourth estate. *Forensic Reports, 3,* 427–437.

Hagen, M. (1997) *Whores of the court: The fraud of psychiatric testimony and the rape of American justice.* New York: HarperCollins.

Haney, C. (1995). The social context of capital murder: Social histories and the logic of mitigation. *Santa Clara Law Review, 35,* 547–609.

Haney, C. (2002, March). *Mitigating evidence.* Panel presentation at the biennial meeting of the American Psychology-Law Society, Austin, TX.

Heilbrun, K. (2002, March). *The importance of feelings in risk communication.* Paper presented at the biennial meeting of the American Psychology-Law Society, Austin, TX.

Hewitt, W. E. (1999, August). Judicial education to help judges understand essential cultural differences. In J. A. McKenna (Chair), *Promotion of social justice—addressing minority issues in psychology and law.* Symposium conducted at the 107th annual convention of the American Psychological Association, Boston.

Hoberman, H. M. (1999). Expert witness report and testimony in sexual predictor civil commitment hearings. In A. Schlank & F. Cohen (Eds.), *The sexual predator: Law, policy, evaluation, and treatment* (Vol. 1, pp. 9.1–9.47). Kingston, NJ: Civic Research Institute.

Hood, L. (2001). *A city possessed: The Christchurch civic crèche case.* Dunedin, New Zealand: Longacre.

Hurwitz, S. D., Miron, M. S., & Johnson, B. T. (1992). Source credibility and the language of expert testimony. *Journal of Applied Social Psychology, 22,* 1909–1939.

Huxley, A. (1937). *Crome yellow.* Garden City, NY: Sun Dial.

Jones, E. E. (1964). *Ingratiation: A social psychological analysis.* New York: Appleton-Century-Crofts.

Kent v. United States, 383 U.S. 541 (1966).

King, S. (1998). *Bag of bones.* New York: Scribner.

Kittrie, N. N. (1971). *The right to be different: Deviance and enforced therapy.* Baltimore: Johns Hopkins University Press.

Marchese, M. C. (1992). Clinical vs. actuarial prediction: A review of the literature. *Perceptual and Motor Skills, 75,* 583–594.

McWhorter, D. (2002). *Carry me home. Birmingham, Alabama: The climactic battle of the civil rights revolution.* New York: Simon & Schuster.

245

Meehl, P. E. (1954). *Clinical versus statistical prediction: A theoretical analysis and a review of the evidence.* Northvale, NJ: Jason Aronson.

Melton, G. B., Petrila, J., Poythress, N. G., & Slobogin, C. (1997). *Psychological evaluations for the courts: A handbook for mental health professionals and lawyers* (2nd ed.). New York: Guilford.

Millon, T., Millon, C., & Davis, R. D. (1994). *Manual for the Millon Clinical Multiaxial Inventory—III.* Minneapolis, MN: National Computer Systems.

Morey, L. C. (1991). *Personality Assessment Inventory: Professional manual.* Lutz, FL: Psychological Assessment Resources.

O'Barr, W. M. (1982). *Linguistic evidence: Language, power, and strategy in the courtroom.* New York: Academic.

O'Connor, M., & Mechanic, M. (2000, June). A broader exploration of the role of gender in expert testimony. Paper presented at the Society for Psychological Study of Social Issues, Ann Arbor, MI.

Parkinson, M. G. (1981). Verbal behavior and courtroom success. *Communication Education, 30,* 22–32.

Parkinson, M. G., Geisler, D., & Pelias, M. H. (1983). The effects of verbal skills on trial success. *Journal of the American Forensic Association, 20,* 16–22.

Pérez-Reverte, A. (1998). The fencing master (M. J. Costa, Trans.). New York: Harcourt.

Quinsey, V., Harris, G., Rice, M., & Cormier, C. (1998). Fifteen arguments against actuarial risk appraisal. In V. Quinsey, G. Harris, M. Rice, & C. Cormier (Eds.), *Violent offenders: Appraising and managing risk* (pp. 171–190). Washington, DC: American Psychological Association.

Rahey, L., & Craig, W. M. (2002). Evaluation of an ecological program to reduce bullying in schools. *Canadian Journal of Counselling, 36,* 281–296.

Rogers, C. R. (1942). *Counseling and psychotherapy: Newer concepts in practice.* Boston: Houghton-Mifflin.

Rogers, C. R. (1951). *Client-centered therapy: Its current practice, implication, and theory.* Boston: Houghton-Mifflin.

Rogers, R. (2000). The uncritical acceptance of risk assessment in forensic practice. *Law and Human Behavior, 24,* 595–605.

Rogers, R., Salekin, R. T., & Sewell, K. W. (1999). Validation of the Millon Clinical Multiaxial Inventory for Axis II disorders: Does it meet the Daubert standard? *Law and Human Behavior, 23,* 425–443.

Rogers, R., Salekin, R. T., & Sewell, K. W. (2000). The MCMI–III and the Daubert standard: Separating rhetoric from reality. *Law and Human Behavior, 24,* 501–506.

Runyon, D. (1944). *The Damon Runyon omnibus.* Garden City, NY: Sun Dial.

Schopp, R. F., Scalora, M. J., & Pearce, M. (1999). Expert testimony and professional judgment: Psychological expertise and commitment as a sexual predator after Hendricks. *Psychology, Public Policy, and Law, 5,* 120–174.

Schopp, R. F., & Sturgis, B. J. (1995). Sexual predators and legal mental illness for civil commitment. *Behavioral Science and the Law, 13,* 437–458.

Silverberg, R. (2001). *Science fiction: 101. Robert Silverberg's worlds of wonder.* New York: ibooks.

Skeem, J. L., Mulvey, E. P., & Lidz, C. W. (2000). Building mental health professionals' decisional models into tests of predictive validity: The accuracy of contextualized predictions of violence. *Law and Human Behavior, 24,* 607–628.

Steinem, G. (1995). *Outrageous acts and everyday rebellions* (2nd ed.). New York: Henry Holt.

Steinem, G. (1994). *Moving beyond words: Age, rage, sex, power, money, muscles: Breaking the boundaries of gender.* New York: Simon & Schuster.

Stengel, R. (2000). *You're too kind: A brief history of flattery.* New York: Simon & Schuster.

Webster, C. D., & Cox, D. (1997). Integration of nomothetic and ideographic positions in risk assessment: Implications for practice and the education of psychologists and other mental health professionals. *American Psychologist, 52,* 1245–1246.

Wellman. F. L. (1936/1997). *The art of cross-examination* (4th ed., rev. and enl.). New York: Touchstone.

Wenhem, M. (2002, July 6). Trials and tribulations. *The Courier-Mail,* Brisbane, Australia, p. 27.

Willshire, D., & Brodsky, S. L. (2001). Toward a taxonomy of unwillingness: Initial steps in engaging the unwilling client. *Psychiatry, Psychology and Law, 8,* 154–160.

About the Author

S TANLEY L. BRODSKY is professor of psychology at the University of Alabama, where he coordinates the Psychology–Law PhD concentration. He is the author of 11 books and 170 articles and chapters, mostly in psychology applied to legal issues. Among other honors, he was the 1996 recipient of the Distinguished Contribution Award for Outstanding Achievement in Forensic Psychology by the American Academy of Forensic Psychology. His books *Testifying in Court: Guidelines and Maxims for the Expert Witness* and *The Expert Expert Witness: More Maxims and Guidelines for Testifying in Court* have become major sourcebooks for expert witnesses. He maintains an independent practice in forensic psychology and is a frequent leader of workshops on court testimony and coping with cross-examination.